NOTES FROM EXILE

NOTES *from* EXILE

On Being Acadian

CLIVE DOUCET

M&S

Canadian Cataloguing in Publication Data

Doucet, Clive, 1946 –
Notes from exile : on being Acadian

ISBN 0-7710-2839-3

1. Doucet, Clive, 1946–   .   2. Acadians – Ethnic identity.
3. Acadians – History.   4. Congres mondial acadien (1994 : Moncton, N.B., and Dieppe, N.B.).   5. Authors, Canadian (English) – 20th century – Biography.*   6. Acadians – Ontario – Ottawa – Biography.   I. Title.

FC2041.D682   1999   971.5'004114   C99-931169-7
FI037.D68   1999

We acknowledge the financial support of the Government of Canada through the Book Publishing Industry Development Program for our publishing activities. Canadä
We further acknowledge the support of the Canada Council for the Arts and the Ontario Arts Council for our publishing program.

Typeset in Goudy by M&S, Toronto
Printed and bound in Canada

McClelland & Stewart Inc.
The Canadian Publishers
481 University Avenue
Toronto, Ontario
M5G 2E9

1 2 3 4 5   03 02 01 00 99

We all travel through life as exiles.
The length and breadth of that voyage
is more apparent to some than others,
but it is always there. We begin life
chased from the womb and finish it
exiled from that selfsame body
in which we began the journey.
The great task given to us all
is to make what sense we can
of that short journey.

CONTENTS

ONE

Beginning

That your lands and tennements, cattle of all Kinds and live
stock of all sorts are forfitted to the crown with all other your
effects, Saving your money and household Goods and you
yourselves to be removed from this his province.

From the deportation order read by Colonel John Winslow in front
of the churches at the villages of Beaubassin, Minas, and Grand-Pré
during the summer of 1755

In August 1755, in the village of Beaubassin, the British navy and a force of two thousand New England militia began the deportation of the Acadian people from what is now Atlantic Canada. The Acadians were the descendants of the first Europeans to settle in North America, the first to have a New World name. They had established themselves in 1604 at Port-Royal in Nova Scotia and by 1755 had grown into a peaceful society of

I

some thirteen thousand souls, surrounding the great Bay of Fundy, which divides Maine and New Brunswick from Nova Scotia. Their economic success was based on a network of dikes they had built to control the high tides in order to convert the miles of natural marshes around the bay into fertile farmland. Politically, they were distinguished by their refusal to bear arms for any of the warring forces around them, French, English, or Indian. This refusal led to catastrophe.

In 1755, just before another declaration of war between France and Britain (Acadie changed hands nine times prior to the Deportation), the Acadians were forced by the British governor, Colonel Charles Lawrence, to leave their communities for resettlement elsewhere. Families were sundered – husbands from wives, children from parents – and the Acadians were sprinkled by the shipload along the coast of the American seaboard, from New England to Louisiana, across the Atlantic to both Britain and France, and as far south as the Falkland Islands. Lawrence's idea was not to exterminate them but to dismantle their communities and sense of themselves as an independent people so that they could never again challenge British interests in North America. It was an eighteenth-century precursor to ethnic cleansing.

In August 1994, Acadians in Atlantic Canada invited Acadians from the worldwide diaspora, the result of the exile of 1755, to come home. A quarter of a million people did. The United Nations called the reunion *the* cultural event of the twentieth century. The Prime Minister of Canada, Jean Chrétien, and the UN Secretary-General, Boutros Boutros-Ghali, attended the opening ceremonies in Moncton, New Brunswick.

News broadcasters from around the world came to record the two-week-long celebration by a people who, without ever fighting, had overcome war, time, oppression, and distance to survive as a people. *Notes from Exile* is a memoir of that reunion and a reflection on the Acadian identity. We are all born human beings but we quickly subdivide into people with different national labels, languages, and traditions. How is it that I came to think of myself as Acadian?

This meditation on identity comes to me naturally because, although my father and his family are Acadian and can trace their roots back to 1632, my mother is a Londoner with all the history, sense of place, and language that implies. All my life I have been confronted with two different personae. I heard the difference every day in the distinctive Acadian accents of my father's voice and the clear vowels of my mother's grammar-school English.

Acadians do not exist in some romantic nirvana. There is no fatherland. The physical homeland of Acadie had already been lost for a hundred years when Longfellow wrote his great poem, *Evangeline*. The sense of being Acadian cannot be separated from the sense of being Canadian or American, English or French, because these identities form both the boundaries and the interstices of the Acadian story. The Acadians are like the Basques in the sense that they have always been a people balanced on the frontier between larger, more powerful national identities.

⬤

When my father joined the RCAF during the Second World War he wrote "Hittite" in the box that requested ethnic origin. It was a story he liked to repeat. When I asked him who the Hittites were he said, "An extinct Middle Eastern people who used to rule a great empire." And then he would laugh. It was one of those tales that children sometimes hear, cannot understand, but lock away in their memories.

Perhaps I would have understood the joke had I known then that my father did have a very clear ethnic origin. He was Acadian. He spoke French in the antique cadence that Acadians have preserved since the seventeenth century. He was close to his family, and I can remember visiting my grandparents on Cape Breton Island from the youngest age, but I cannot remember my father ever making any reference to being anything other than Canadian. He could have been Hittite. It was as if the culture and history that had formed him had disappeared from his consciousness.

One summer evening, after I had left home, I saw a play called *La Sagouine*, by the great Acadian writer Antonine Maillet. It is about an Acadian washerwoman who is approaching the end of her life. There are no other characters except La Sagouine talking about her life, and no props except for a stool, a bucket of water, and a mop. Yet it is one of those tidal, defining works that appear only once in a great while to illuminate not just one person's life, but the heartbeat of a people.

La Sagouine's stories are of an Acadie few see or hear who are not born into it. When the play first came to Grand Étang, my father's village in Cape Breton, my aunt went to see it at the local school. By chance, I was visiting from university. I asked if I could go along too, and my aunt replied in an embarrassed way, "No, no, it's just a foolish thing about an old woman," implying that I would be wasting my valuable, educated time on nonsense. My aunt is a powerful woman. I followed her advice and did not go.

It was not until many years later, long after *La Sagouine* had become a great hit in Québec and France, that I actually saw the play. It is a drama about the simplest and most complex of things – work, marriage, love, dancing, God, hope, and despair – all told in the accents and vocabulary of Acadie.

At one point in the play, La Sagouine wonders about her sense of nationality. Who is she? What is she? This reflection is sparked by the arrival in the mail of a Canadian census form with a box marked "ethnic origin," just as my father's response of "Hittite" was sparked by an Armed Forces recruiting document form asking for his ethnic origin:

Is La Sagouine American?
No, Americans are rich.

Is she French?
I feel less French than American.
Canadian?
I can't be one of them. Besides, they're English.
Canadien?
Those are the people that live in Québec.
Is she Acadian?
They didn't want to write this word on their census list. Someone must have told them Acadie is not a country. I think they have put us in the box with the Indians.

La Sagouine is talking about nothing less than the disappearance of a people from the geography of nations. In that moment I saw not just the connection between her and my father, but all the connections that I had been surrounded by all my life but could not discern. It was as if a window had been blown open by a sudden wind and a vista had appeared that I had never seen before. For the first time, I understood the point of my father's joke about being a Hittite. He was saying exactly the same thing. Like La Sagouine, my father felt himself to be Acadian but he could not bring himself to write it on the form, so he'd written Hittite, choosing an ancient culture which once had place and importance in the world but no longer did. In that moment, I began to get an inkling of the great conflict he must have felt all his life. He was Acadian. Old Acadian French was his first language. Until his eighteenth year, his life had been surrounded by the intense and busy life of an isolated Acadian village. Yet, Acadie no longer existed. It had disappeared at gunpoint. He could not write Acadian on the recruiting form.

———— • ————

From the youngest age, there were two poles of attraction in my life, English from my mother's side and Acadian from my father's. The Acadian world was always vibrant and exciting because my father had seven brothers and two sisters. I had more cousins than I would ever meet, and there were always great comings and goings as members of the family whooshed in and out of the house. It was a world in a whirl around the little village of Grand Étang, but its exact importance and place in the world remained mysterious to me. The Doucets were French speaking but not French like the French-French. We were Canadian but not Canadian like the English speakers either, and these confusions eddied gently about the edges of my young life. In a vague way, I thought the Montréal Canadiens were mostly Acadian because they spoke French, and that they played in Montréal because Montréal was big.

There was never any confusion of place and importance when I visited my English grandparents. Here, the boundaries of nations and the marks of history were clear. There was the matter of passports and customs officers and gateways. It wasn't hard to understand that Britain was a nation and London was its great capital. Almost as soon as I was able to read, I absorbed more than learned the succession of English kings and queens from the mythical King Arthur to the young Queen Elizabeth II.

When my parents sent me to Grandfather Doucet's, there were no kings or queens or empires to be recalled. My father just said, "Remember you are Clive à Fernand à William à Arsène à Magloire." That was all I needed to know to my place in the village. From this everyone would know I was the son of Fernand who had gone away to university, and the grandson of William who had the farm on the hill about a mile from the harbour, and great-grandson of Arsène who had died at sea, and great-great grandson of Magloire. No one ever told me that the first Doucet was named Germain and had arrived in 1632 at Port-Royal, or that I had Mi'kmaq great-grandmothers. The long, rich, complicated tapestry of Acadian history was unspoken and unacknowledged.

In 1994, my trip to the Retrouvailles was just part of a larger voyage that I have been taking all my life. It was a voyage inspired not so much by what was there, but what was not there. I would return home from summers in Grand Étang and the French teacher would feel obliged to correct my accent and clean up my vocabulary. Only years later did I realize that "*mover*" was old Norman French and not an anglicism. It never occurred to me to question my teachers. Similarly, I took it for granted that Acadian history was an insignificant blip when almost four centuries of history was glossed over with something like: "In 1755, at the outbreak of the colonial war, the neutral, French-speaking inhabitants of Nova Scotia were deported." I learned that the real history of Canada began in Québec with such famous figures as Samuel de Champlain, and that modern Canada started in 1867 with Confederation and Sir John A. Macdonald. This was all that was taught. As La Sagouine said, "We were with the Indians."

Leaving the boundaries of my grandfather's village was like crossing an invisible, impermeable frontier. On one side, there was one language, history, dance, music, one way of viewing the world and relating to people, and on the other side was another. Nor was there any way that I could explain either world to anyone once I had crossed the boundary. Once my Uncle Philias had driven me from the village to the airport at Sydney to take the plane home, Grand Étang disappeared. There was no way of explaining it to any of my school friends or of having it explained to me. If I had been able to tell my teachers that Acadie still existed, that there were still people in Canada who carried on their lives in a way that went back to the exile – and beyond that exile to the Acadie of legend and *Evangeline* – it might have been of interest in an exotic sense, but it would have been irrelevant.

In my Larousse, under the name Port-Royal, there are two entries. The first is a description of an important convent in France called Port-Royal. The second is about a literary/political movement also called Port-Royal. End of entries under Port-Royal. There is no mention of Port-Royal, the New World village where Acadie began.

These *Notes From Exile* were originally written to myself, to the young boy who once felt much but understood little, who would drive down to the harbour in the buggy with his grandfather, who felt another world in the turning of a day. These are my notes from the disappearance.

T W O

Available Space

I've already stopped worrying. Now I come back with bread and cheese. Emile is still sunbathing on the letter Z. Girls play the harp in his eyes, a marbled poem slides down along his leg. Over him, while former lovers nearly die with laughter, electric trains climb up rainbows.

Dyane Léger, Poet, Notre Dame de Kent

I have just crossed the Québec border. I am waiting at the information counter at the New Brunswick tourist office for my turn to get highway directions. There is no reason for me to be nervous. A family reunion shouldn't be anything to be anxious about, but I can feel tension vibrating through me. At the back of my mind, I'm wondering what the hell I am doing. I probably won't know a soul. No one from my immediate family is going. There's no real reason why they should.

The Doucets of Grand Étang had a family reunion in 1993 in the village. I stayed with my parents and sister at the Levert's old house, one of the very few in the village that was virtually unchanged from the 1930s. An indoor toilet and some rudimentary electric lights were the only modern amenities. The kitchen was heated with a wood-stove and the furniture was the same as in my father's childhood. Six children grew up here. My grandfather's house was a little grander but much the same. My most powerful memory of his house is of the simplicity of every-thing. There was nothing that was not needed or used: handmade chairs, cupboards, a kitchen table for cooking and eating. I always found this soothing, not austere. There was a place for everything and everything had a place.

Francis Levert was a great friend of my father's youth. They were close in the way only teenagers can be, full of exuberance and exaltation. There is a photo of the two of them in front of the old house wearing their first suits; two very cool, very skinny eighteen-year-olds on their way to a serious social. It makes me smile. In their day, their suits probably inspired violent envy, but the passage of time renders everything quaint.

The Levert house was built by Francis's father, who was a shipwright, and everything is constructed as if for a boat. The stairs are pitched as steep as a gangway and the bedrooms are like cabins. You must bend a little to look out the windows. It feels as if you are staring out of a port-hole. It's comical, and people in the village always smile when they think of the Levert's old house, but being inside is as calming as being on a wooden boat as it makes its way slowly over the planet. The house was exactly as my father remembers.

The days in Grand Étang passed gently. I had rarely seen my father so relaxed. He is a man who has travelled and lived through wars, earned university degrees, learned several languages. There are few corners of the world that he has not visited, and he uses these experiences like a shield to deflect conversations into avenues he can control. But it was different here. From the Levert's house he could see where he was born. In the morning, cows meandered by the kitchen window on their way to the hill pasture, like terrestrial whales. A rooster crowed a final time to signal that the sun had risen. Patrick Levert and his brother chatted by the tractor in the wonderful, archaic accents of Acadie. It was the sound of home. I could sense my father laying down his shield.

At the Doucet reunion, in the parish hall, I tried not to think of how fragile the older generation was becoming. I remembered them all in their vigorous middle age, when they hustled about the village trying to do more than could reasonably be done in one day. They were still with us, but fainter, as if they had become observers of their former selves. It spooked me as if Father Time were treading on my own grave.

My son and daughter have grown up in a family with two working parents. They can't imagine what it is like to have ten children under one roof and more cousins than you can remember. But I am old enough to remember when my uncles and aunts were young and the Doucet family was a great jumble of brothers, sisters, and cousins. I am old enough to remember making my first set of downhill skis by hand, screwing in the steel edges piece by piece, painting on the base, setting the binding. Money has always been important, but in the 1950s it didn't have the overwhelming significance that it does now. I can't imagine any youngster today using homemade skis; the social discomfort would be suffocating. Nor can I imagine children spending the entire summer at their grandparents'. Summers are for canoe and computer camps and various other improving outings.

I looked around the parish hall and I felt the history not just of my family but of the whole village, because the two are meshed like the squares of a fisherman's net. Our farm lay between Arthur Leblanc's and Peter à Joe Chiasson. There were long, common fences between the three properties. Lives, marriages, work, all interconnected. Arthur Leblanc was a carpenter and a farmer. Peter à Joe was a fisherman who kept a cow and a garden. In the blink of an eye, I can see myself as a child, sitting in John à Joe's garden while he braided a rope halter for my grandfather's prize calf. His strong, brown hands wove the strands together so quickly that the new halter emerged like magic from what minutes earlier had been a few strands of hemp. I remember his quick smile and shrug as he passed it to me. It was easy for him. He could make anything with fibre – fishing nets, sweaters, harnesses. His was not a global world. It was a village world. Among my grandfather, a farmer, Peter à Joe, a fisherman, and Arthur, a carpenter, there was a complicity and a confidence that I have seen among few other people. Yet they had no money to speak of and little formal education.

I am twelve. I am standing in Grand Étang, in front of Grandfather's house, which overlooks the great arc of the sea and sky. My cousin Roland is coming to see me, his cousin from the city. Roland is nine and he's bouncing up and down behind the steering wheel of his father's dump truck with a great grin on his face. It takes me a few seconds to realize that he's sitting on his father's knee because he's too small to steer and work the pedals at the same time. My friendship with Roland has always been tinged with the awe I felt on seeing such an early accomplishment.

It is easy to dismiss the connection between the Acadie of *Evangeline* and the Acadie of my grandfather, so many things changed irrevocably. Farming behind large sea dikes, the mainstay of old Acadie, was unknown in Cape Breton. Old Acadie didn't have a clerical culture, years went by without any priests at all and Catholicism became a lay religion, leavened with strong doses of Mi'kmaq spirituality and Huguenot Protestantism. It was only after Acadians regrouped in fishing villages in the remote reaches of Maritime Canada that missionaries brought them into the main Catholic stream and their religion became as institutionalized as it was in Québec, with priests, bishops, dioceses, approved liturgy, and ritual.

In the confusion of the exile, the meaning of secular festivals such as the Tintamarre was lost. Saddest of all, the old friendships and family relations with the Mi'kmaq people were shattered and forgotten. Now, there is a move to revive the Tintamarre, a midsummer festival during which people come out of their homes and parade down Main Street, banging and clanging pots and pans. But its raison d'être is lost. It's a mystery.

My sense, nonetheless, is that many of the intangibles – the attitudes, beliefs, the values that define how people go about their lives – did survive the exile. The documents of nations – citizenship certificates, passports – are new requirements, no more than a few centuries old. Before there were nations and passports, before there were feudal kingdoms, there were just people. And throughout time people have lived within the landscape of shared memory, the geography of living places, in the organization of kin lines, in the poetry of work, love, language, and the daily round between sunrise and sunset.

Working together to build ocean dikes is a thing of the past, but community projects are still central to Acadian life. Most of the major economic and social institutions of Acadian villages are co-operatives; there are co-op fish plants, co-op credit unions, stores, theatres, workshops, historical societies, radio stations. On Prince Edward

Island there are only about six thousand French-speaking Acadians left, but there are twelve Acadian co-operative societies. Curiously, at the same time that these co-operatives flourish, so do private enterprise and private endeavour. This is how it has always been among Acadians. Historical records show a great willingness to build dikes together, but also a great willingness to get litigious about who owned what. The dikes were not communal property once they were built. Individual farmers owned them and they defended their property rights vigorously.

In writing *Evangeline*, Longfellow was not troubled by historical accuracy, but the facts dispute his pastoral vision. A good deal of the farmland around Beaubassin (Sackville, today), the single largest farming area in old Acadie, lay fallow at the time of the exile because Acadians were arguing over who owned what. And Acadians haven't changed. Their farms are private, as are their fishing boats and sheds. As a boy, I caught hell from a fisherman for walking on his wharf without asking permission.

Property still has strict boundaries, and so do families. The Doucets are the Doucets; the Cormiers, the Cormiers; the Leblancs, the Leblancs; the Chiassons, the Chiassons; and so on, each with a distinct character. The Doucets have always been famous for their energy; one job isn't enough. Uncle Philias was a mechanic and a schoolteacher, and was content only when he was both teaching school and fixing cars. Grandfather harnessed horses, milked cows, ploughed and planted, and kept his little farm going long after most men had retired. Grandmother had her last child at age forty-eight.

An apocryphal Doucet story is of Uncle Gérard carrying up all the shingles to the top stage of the scaffolding for the roofers before he left for his own work. When the roofers arrived and couldn't find the shingles on the ground, comically, they complained someone had stolen them. This story went the rounds in the village until everyone had heard it and laughed.

Aunt Germaine has always been a lightly harnessed whirlwind. All her energy goes into words; listening to her rapid-fire voice is like braving a southeast verbal storm. It is as if we Doucets have been bitten by the devil and can never sit down except to get up. The only exception was my cousin Marcel, the fiddler. Marcel played all over Cape Breton, in Upper Canada, even in Scotland. But he was not one who needed two jobs. When he wasn't playing the fiddle, he passed the day with his feet up in quiet contemplation of the planet's rotation.

His younger brother, Robert, has five children and usually at least three jobs at once. His older sisters are married and have both jobs and families to care for. Marcel never married and liked children to stay on the horizon. Everyone loved Marcel but in the family, people shook their heads when his name came up, as if the words Marcel and Doucet were joined uneasily. He only had one job.

At the reunion, I overheard my father telling a story about Francis Levert and himself. In the 1930s, people were poor and meals did not vary much from home to home. On Friday, it was fish and on Saturday, it was beans and pork. After battering through their homework on Saturday, Francis would say to my father, "Well, shall we try the beans at your house or my house tonight?" My father laughed when he told the story. Both he and Francis have since travelled all over the world. Francis ended up in Vancouver, Dad in Ottawa, but neither of them ever found another place where they could say such a simple thing to a friend.

On the negative side of the Doucets à William à Arsène, there is a certain prickliness, a stiff-neckedness that some say is characteristic of all Acadians and which the Doucet family has in spades. We are not a family that accepts help gracefully. In Louisiana, there is a joke that goes, "You can tell a Cajun a mile off, but you can't tell him a damn thing close up." I felt that stiffness in the Grand Étang parish hall. A stranger wouldn't have noticed it for all the talk, laughter, and loud voices, but it was there underneath the conversation. I saw it in my younger cousins as well as in the older generation. It is written in the way we hold ourselves, as if waiting for bad weather to arrive.

Fortunately, there is also a quixotic dimension to the Doucet character which leavens the stiffness, otherwise we would be insufferable. In 1879, my great-grandfather, Arsène Doucet, built a merry-go-round for a parish picnic, the first one that had ever been seen in the district. No one knows where he got this frivolous idea or why he worked so hard to build it, but the fun the children had is remembered. My great-great-grandfather, Magloire Doucet, built his house right on the edge of the cliff so that the ships passing by could see it like a lighthouse. He is remembered as a non-believer, fearing neither God nor the English. I don't know about the English, but it's said there was a steady stream of missionaries at his door.

In the parish hall, some of the children began to step-dance. No one knows if step-dancing was part of old Acadie, but my earliest memories are of people step-dancing in our kitchen. Sometimes there was no fiddle, just a voice sounding out the rhythms of the tune perfectly. Moccasined feet swishing on the bare floor counterpointed the music like brush strokes on a snare drum, till the dancing and the playing reached a crescendo. Waves against the shore.

In my dreams, I am a great fiddle player, able, like Ashley MacIsaac, to step-dance and play at the same time. I am laughing and a girl is dancing with me. We are dancing at the Chandeleur festival, and we are immortal.

My cousin Roland came to the reunion; Roland the star – class valedictorian, excellent athlete, guitarist, speaks both French and English impeccably. We always thought he would end up as the MP for Inverness after a stint running his own business, but it didn't work out that way. After university, Roland found conventional life too confining and decamped for New Orleans, where he played in a blues band

and waited tables. He's hitchhiked around the planet with his guitar over his shoulder, worked as a carpenter, a union rep, and now for an MP. He's the cousin I know the best.

Roland made his way around the room like a politician meeting and greeting *le monde*. He had a smile and a story for everyone. I watched him measuring people, appraising me. How had I changed? How was the long, wiry man I have become related to the kid Roland once knew? I seem to have weathered the years as much as lived them; time has sculpted my face into a craggy visage that shows my soul close to the surface. Roland still has the aura of the boy who once steered his father's truck down the farm lane; he is as easy with himself and others as he was then.

Roland's dad, Gérard, and our uncle Alex belong to the generation that Acadian historians call *l'Acadie de la survivance*, an Acadie that was isolated from the outside world, still carrying the exile not far from its collective memory. Gérard and Alex were the closest to my grandfather, and the sense of Acadie hung about them and my grandfather the same way that a Mi'kmaq elder carries the sense of the Mi'kmaq culture. They needed no books to teach them what it meant to be Acadian. They were Acadie.

My father was born at the other end of the family, and although only about ten years separates him from his older brothers, it is as if he is from another generation. His contemporaries fought in the Second World War, became university educated, and instead of looking out at the world from the village, looked from the world back at the village.

My father became one of the federal civil servants who helped to modernize the old handline fishery with long liners, freezer plants, harbour works, and different ideas about marketing.

I'm not sure which view has been the hardest, the view from the village or of the village. Gérard and Alex certainly had to work physically harder than my father. They built their own houses, their own barns, they ploughed the land, worked in the woods, drove trucks, bought and sold things. In a little village, a living has to be cobbled together by long hours and many activities. But my father's journey was also hard. There was no path cut out for him when he left the village and entered the jostling, competitive, larger world; there was no father or older brother holding a door open for him. He had to push them all open by himself and, from time to time, he found it overwhelming. Times have changed, and I know it is difficult for my children to understand what a struggle it was for their grandfather. I remember my mother telling me that when she and my father first came to Ottawa with two young children, my father did not speak English as well as he thought he should, and the terrible thought crossed her mind: At least he's not black.

The Acadie of Gérard and Alex was different from my father's and different again from mine. Gérard and Alex can remember the last Chandeleur parties held in the village. La Chandeleur festival goes back to old Acadie. It is held at that time in the Catholic calendar after Christmas has been digested and before the Lenten season starts its earnest slide towards Easter. Although over the years it has acquired a faint religious dimension, when on the Sunday the priest blesses the candles, the reality is La Chandeleur is one of those great Celtic festivals that never fully made the transition to being a Holy Day of the Catholic church. The lighting of the Chandeleur candles to calm stormy seas has a magical rather than a religious quality. At bottom, La Chandeleur belonged to Bacchus; the priest had good reason to be suspicious of it as an "occasion for sin" and the people good reason to love it.

The "occasion for sin" would begin with a group of young men driving horsedrawn sleighs from house to house to collect food. The leader danced with a beribboned cane at each house and sang an old song called "L'Escaouette," the words of which came from both the Mi'kmaq language and the exile. When the song was over, the leader asked for contributions for the party. It was a rare house that did not donate a pie, a loaf of bread, something to fill the Chandeleur tables. Later that night the village gathered, and the dancing and story-telling lasted as long as the food, drink, and the fiddlers did – which meant until the sun came up and sometimes longer.

Chandeleur or no Chandeleur, the Doucets à William à Arsène dressed for church as if for inspection. Everything had to be just right, suits pressed, ties knotted, hair combed, shoes shined, and they all had such terrible, wonderful smiles, it doesn't surprise me that my mother found them intimidating. She was the only child of a very English family where three people sat quietly at the dining-room table for meals, and in case of rain, umbrellas were kept carefully furled in the hall stand. Meeting her Cape Breton in-laws for the first time must have been like surfacing on a different planet after a long, deep dive. Nor would meeting the women of the Doucet family have been reassuring.

Acadian women are not backwards about coming forward. They like to talk with big voices and their French is peppered with rich, antique images. They have an opinion on everything and an opinion for everyone. They like to manage. They like to be in charge. I suspect old Acadie, if not a matriarchy, was *égal à égal.* It is no accident that the heroes of Acadie are all women: Evangeline, La Sagouine, Pélagie-la-Charette. My image of Acadian women is of my aunts Lucy-May, Annie, Germaine, Bernadette. Of that generation, the women were better educated than the men. My grandmother had her provincial leaving certificate. My grandfather could not read or write. It was my grandmother who dealt with the paper that flowed in the front door from the government, from the parish, from the co-op. Lucy-May did the same thing for Gérard, carefully correcting the spelling of his name every time the provincial civil servants in Halifax misspelt it. In the village, all the men were henpecked. Everyone knew William à Arsène was henpecked. Everyone knew Gérard à William was henpecked, and so on. The truth was they had typical Acadian marriages in which there was a complicated, caring intimacy between the partners. Uncle

Gérard was not quick to voice his opinion on any subject, but when he told a story people listened. To the outsider, he may have seemed henpecked. But there was an understanding between Gérard and Lucy-May. Lucy-May would always look to her husband to see where he stood and if it wasn't clear, she waited until they could talk away from watching eyes.

At our family reunion, everything had slowed down. It was as if the camera were running at the wrong speed. Uncle Gérard had had a stroke. He still had his wonderful smile and warm, brown eyes, but he moved slowly, spoke hesitantly, recalled things slowly. Aunt Lucy-May still had her disconcerting ability to know exactly what you were thinking before you knew it yourself, but her eyes were worried and often strayed to her husband.

Uncle Alex, the eldest, in his eighties and still driving his car, watched everything calmly with his bright, evaluating intelligence, measuring people's character the way a tailor measures the body for a suit. I think all store owners end up doing this; it comes with the trade. They see the avaricious and the generous in the daily human parade in a way that few others do. Alex's dry wit missed nothing, but at the reunion he was quiet as if he was sitting up in a tree watching the parade pass by beneath. He started selling from a horse and cart in the 1930s, when people bought things just for the sake of the conversation and news. Later, he built up a small store on the edge of Chéticamp; he passed it on to his second son, Robert. He saw both daughters leave for the city and buried both his wife and his eldest son, the Cape Breton fiddler, Marcel Doucet. But none of this bent him to the earth; instead it seemed to have burnished him. His sense of humour remained dry and wicked. Uncle Alex is that magical kind of man who is moral without being sententious. For many of his nephews and nieces he has been a model.

After years of ferocious walking, Aunt Germaine's legs quit on her and she now uses a wheelchair. The wild bursts of static seemed to have calmed to ordinary conversation. Her thick, jet black hair had condensed like a dwarf star to a grey-white cap. Aunt Germaine was always an unfinished work. She would rage against the unfairness of life in a way that pulverised everyone around her. And then from time to time, a sweet spirit would escape as if all else was an encumbering cloud. Germaine's storms are burned in my soul, but so are her moments of flight. I remember walking across the fields with her to Gérard à Levis's house. It was high summer and the sun was setting in the sea, the mountain pastures gentle with the soft perfumes of the harvest. At moments like this, Aunt Germaine chattered like a small bird escaped from a cage. Her storms calmed, her spirit delighted. But at the reunion I was as cautious around her as ever, watching my words.

What I remember most from the family reunion is not the toll of years, nor the stories, nor the view of the countryside from the Levert's old house. What I remember is the love. It was like a great wave that kept rolling across the parish hall, burying all old family irritations, leaving only the residue of affection and shared efforts which has sustained brothers and sisters, nephews and nieces, *cousins* and *cousines* over the years in their travels, in their ambitions and their troubles.

The children played one of Marcel's fiddle tunes, "Available Space." Marcel had just started to write down his tunes before he died. "Available Space" is a not a complicated tune, but it has become popular with fiddlers because it combines both traditional qualities and the more open sound of modern music. It is a tune that sails, and there are a lot of damp eyes as the notes unfold.

I found myself biting at the inside of my lip, uncomfortable with the sudden sure feeling that this would be the last family reunion for the Doucets à William à Arsène. Grandfather's farm had been sold and broken up into suburban, village plots. The Doucets of the next century will have no farm in Grand Étang to visit or remember. It felt to me as if the Acadie of my grandfather, of my father, uncles, and aunts had slipped into memory, that we were now all on different shores, looking at different horizons.

Going to this Retrouvailles is not the same thing at all. It is not just the reunion of one family from one small village, it is the reunion of all the families of Acadie from all over the world. It seems an impossible ambition. How can you reunite thousands of people who happen to carry the same names? Will we have anything in common? Is it not a presumptuous thing to do?

It will be difficult just finding my way around. The guidebook to the Retrouvailles is the size of a telephone directory and as cramped as an airline schedule. It consists of pages and pages of family reunions, dances, films, plays, concerts, barbecues, literary events, craft sales, conferences, the list goes on and on. I can't make head or tail of it. I have the unsettling feeling that I will spend two weeks in New Brunswick and come home wondering why I went. But the audacity of bringing together Acadians from the four corners of the world, from all the distant shores that we have ended up on, in one place at one time remains enormously appealing. It has never been tried before, and I want to go just to see if there is a place where I fit.

THREE

Leaf on the Water

*In 1604 there aren't any Acadians; they don't exist. By 1713
there are people who say, "Je suis Acadien." So what interests me is how a group of people come together – because there
is nothing in those who come to Acadie to make them
Acadian; they are formed here – bringing their European heritage in a way that reacts to the North American situation to
make themselves Acadian, and then to make this an enduring
sense of identity.*

Naomi Griffiths, Professor Emeritus, History, Carleton University

There are two older women at the information
counter just in front of me. They are bending over
a road map with the clerk, who is drawing a line
from the Québec border down the Trans-Canada Highway
to a village on the coast. I can't help but notice that it is

the same place that I am going to, and I ask if we could get directions together. They smile and agree.

I soon learn that these two women are also Doucets, also on their way to the family reunion in Richibucto. One is from Montréal, the other from Ottawa. The woman from Montréal says that she grew up in Newcastle, New Brunswick, "where Doucets are common as flies on the wall." She laughs when she says this. From a file she is carrying, she pulls out a document. It is a copy of the birth certificate of Urbain Doucet, the brother of Germain Doucet, from La Chaussé, France, dated September 8, 1600. Captain Germain Doucet was the first Doucet to arrive in the New World in 1632 at Port-Royal. His name is mixed up with all the early Acadian adventures, in the grinding civil war between Charles de Menou d'Aulnay and Charles La Tour, and in the war with the Bostonnais.

It was Germain Doucet who was forced to strike the French colours at Port-Royal in 1654 in the face of the English assault from Boston. He returned to France in a huff with his soldiers, his arms, and his flags flying. But his children stayed, and it is from his son and his Mi'kmaq wife that my branch of the family is descended. The little document announcing the birth of his brother, Urbain, is written in both Latin and French. The script is decorated everywhere with spiralling lines, each word sending off curls into the next. It is more a ceremonial declaration of status than a simple description of birth.

The woman from Montréal tells me her father could not read. "We were poor as church mice. I left home with one cardboard suitcase and not much in it." Tears well in her eyes as she remembers.

Her name is Norah Doucet-Fishman, and she is travelling to the Retrouvailles with her cousin. She insists on calling me cousin also. We are all talking a mile a minute. We keep switching from French to English and back again. No one seems to be able to settle, and it strikes me suddenly that they are as nervous as I am. They are also wondering how they will fit in.

We spread the old document over the hood of their car, along with maps of Canada and France. Little by little, we calm down. Soon, we are mulling over the paper, trying to decipher exactly what it says. It isn't easy. The Latin and the French are both written in convoluted, archaic, ecclesiastical jargon. Norah tells me she found the original in a church in France, and the priest gave it to her without batting an eye. She was a Doucet. There were no longer any Doucets in the parish. Why shouldn't she have it? Norah says that as she took it she had the impression of the hand of fate launching a paper airplane across time.

I understand what she means. The existence of the little document in our hands has the feel of cosmic laughter. After all, what is four centuries? In the turn of planetary life, not much more than the blink of an eye, yet so much has happened. People no longer take months crossing the ocean on sailing ships. Educated people no longer read Latin; it has become a dead language in written as well as spoken form. And our ancestor, Captain Germain Doucet, who once had a brother called Urbain, who once had two children called Pierre and Marguerite, who once defended Port-Royal and felt the smash of cannon balls against his wooden fort, who cradled friends in his arms as they died in this vast new world, who once was alive to all the connections, excitement, and tenderness that life for human beings implies, has become a curious genealogical icon, like an old coin from a bygone culture that once meant something but is now just a disk of worn metal. And the New World, to which Germain Doucet devoted so much of his life, a place of innumerable Indian nations and vast populations, has mutated into something else, into something more complex and infinitely less splendid, with gas stations and highways and the bloat of too many defeated dreams. Then this little baptismal paper floats from the past towards us like a leaf on the water, reminding us that our own destinies are no mightier than this distant ancestor's, our lifespans no grander.

Norah has a map of France and on it you can still find the little village of La Chaussé in the Loire Valley, where Urbain Doucet was born. All the time, we are laughing and talking, delighted to have found each other, bits and pieces of our lives floating to the surface.

My retrouvailles have begun.

FOUR

Frogs and Limies

It's an exile in eighteenth-century conditions, which are god-awful. The supplies are adequate, they're better than those given to British troops shipped to North America, but they're not brilliant. If the ship is delayed, they're going to run short of water, they're going to run short of food. Somewhere between a third and half of those loaded die before they are landed. And those that make it are off-loaded into camps. Now, these aren't concentration camps like Bergen-Belsen, they are just ordinary camps, but these camps are swept by disease, small pox, cholera, measles, all those things. So there's a second great death toll that goes through the camps after landing.

Naomi Griffiths, Professor Emeritus, History, Carleton University

After the Québec border, the Trans-Canada Highway narrows to two lanes, and the road becomes clogged with holiday travellers in camping caravans of every description. Cars loaded with bicycles and tents, children and dogs sway along the road. Mixed in with these holidayers, who have the raucous, sunburnt quality of beach pilgrims, are enormous trucks laden with logs or containers, straining up hills only to lurch down the other side at high speed. It isn't easy driving. Locals have the tendency to turn casually onto the highway in their half-tons as if it is their own laneway, disregarding the evidence that the road is awash in fast-moving vehicles. The Saint John River Valley is a gentle, rolling place, which seems independent of the great continent it is part of – a world unto itself.

In Québec, the Trans-Canada is dominated along its entire route by the St. Lawrence. The river is never far away and its enormous size, like an inland freshwater sea, diminishes the road within the vaster scale of the continent. It is easy to understand why General Wolfe felt intimidated by the landscape and unequal to the task before him. The St. Lawrence and the Mississippi are the two great arteries of the continent. They drain and nourish vast areas. Following the broad back of the Mississippi up from the Gulf of Mexico gives the traveller the same sense of inextricable connection to the heart of the continent as the St. Lawrence conveys.

Maritime Canada is a different, softer place. Dairy and potato farms line the edges of the road. The rivers and valleys are smaller, and there is a sense of descending to the sea. The roadside restaurants sell home-baked pies, date squares, biscuits, and cold milk fresh from the dairy, which is never far away. The taste is pure pleasure. At Bathurst and Edmunston, I hear Acadian voices at the restaurant counter, and I drink in the roll of the old accent as if I were parched.

It begins to rain, a light, steady drizzle, and the traffic slows. I come over a ridge and discover a car that has been eaten by a truck. Apparently the truck driver hit his brakes but was unable to stop in time, and his truck slid on the wet pavement, up and over the car. The entire back of the sedan is crushed. The cab of the truck is resting on top of what is left of it. The curious thing is that the front seat of the car is absolutely untouched. From the front, it looks like an ordinary car, only, the back half no longer exists. Fortunately, no harm seems to have been done to the passengers. There is no sign of an ambulance and people are just milling around the edge of the accident chatting.

The woman at the information desk has marked my route off clearly enough. I am to follow the Trans-Canada to Fredericton, and once east of Fredericton, I must turn north and slightly east to go up to Moncton, where the academic side of the Retrouvailles will be held. Moncton is named after the British Colonel Monckton, who was in charge of deportation of the Acadians. It is one of history's little ironies that the town named after him has become the hotbed of the modern Acadian revival.

It always amazes me how young these soldiers were. Robert Monckton was only twenty-nine when Colonel Lawrence chose him to lead the attack on Fort Beauséjour and direct the deportation of the Acadians. Four years later, in 1759, Monckton was at Québec as General Wolfe's second-in-command. Monckton belongs to that long line of British soldier–civil servants who changed Britain's position in the world, whether the king or Parliament wanted it changed or not. It was men such as he who made Britain a world power.

In 1755, Monckton had three hundred regular British soldiers under his direct command and two thousand militiamen from New England. The young militia officers from Boston would do most of the work. John Winslow from Boston was in charge of the deportation at Beaubassin and later at Grand-Pré. He reminds me of the young American soldiers this century who went to Vietnam with high ideals of defending democracy and their country, only to see them dissolve in what became apparent was neither a noble nor a just endeavour. Winslow kept a journal, and it begins with entries in Boston replete with schoolboy enthusiasm about the "great and noble adventure" that he and his compatriots are embarked on "to remove the French neutrals who have always been our secret enemies and have encouraged the Indians to slit our throats." He was twenty-five.

The reality was different. The Acadians had steadfastly refused to take an oath of allegiance that would require them to participate in the fighting between the British and French. They remained neutral. When asked to, they gave up their guns and boats without resistance. Their attention was focussed on the summer hay harvest on which they and their animals would depend for the coming winter. Soldiers were billeted near Acadian villages without incident.

The siege of the French fort of Beauséjour was not very glorious and did not last long. The fort was manned by about a hundred regular French soldiers, and was quickly surrounded, out-gunned and overwhelmed by the Boston militia. It fell on June 16, 1755, after two weeks. Inside the fort, Colonels Monckton and Winslow discovered three hundred young Acadian men who had battled alongside the French troops in the fort's defence. Commandant Vergor presented the English colonels with a document saying that the Acadians had been conscripted. It was ignored. This was the excuse that Colonel Lawrence had long been waiting for to justify his plan to deport the Acadians to English colonies, where they would be a minority and could be quietly assimilated.

The Deportation began. At each village, Winslow read the deportation order, which had been written by Lawrence, from the church steps. It stripped the Acadians of everything but what they could carry: "That your lands and tennements, cattle of all Kinds and live stock of all sorts are forfitted to the crown with all other your effects, Saving your money and household Goods and you yourselves to be removed from this his province."

In his diary, we start to see Winslow's disenchantment with his "noble" endeavour. Just prior to issuing the first deportation order he said to the people gathered before the church: "The part of duty I am now upon is what tho[h] necessary is Very Disagreeable to my natural make & Temper, as I Know it Must be Grievous to you who are of the Same specia."

As a precautionary measure against a resistance forming, the Acadian men were separated from the women and sometimes put on different ships. In this way, many families were divided forever because the ships did not arrive at the same destination. From this circumstance arose the story of a young couple being separated on their wedding day, only to be reunited years later at his deathbed. This story was the raw material for Longfellow's poem *Evangeline*.

Winslow begins his journal of the Deportation at the village of Beaubassin on August 11, 1755. The village was not much more than a cannon shot from the French fort of Beauséjour, and it was the village from which my ancestor, Paul-Marie Doucet, fled. He was eight years old. His experience was typical of the time. Beaubassin was burnt, all the animals confiscated, and Paul-Marie was separated from his family. It is not known what happened to the parents, and what happened to him for the next twenty years is a mystery, but he seems to have evaded the deportation ships. The best guess is that he lived with the Mi'kmaq. Years later, his older brother washed up in Louisiana after living in the La Rochelle refugee camps in France. He had heard that Paul-Marie was in the Miramichi region of New Brunswick.

When he was around the age of thirty, Paul-Marie and his wife, Felicity-Michel, surfaced at Chéticamp on Cape Breton Island. Felicity has no maiden name in the record of her marriage, and from this it is assumed she was Mi'kmaq.

By the fall of 1755, Winslow had had enough. He wrote to Colonel Lawrence that he did not want to continue his part in the deportation at Port-Royal. His "noble endeavour" had collapsed. I like John Winslow and can easily imagine the disintegration of his heroic schoolboy visions to the point of his wanting only to go home. Boys raised on stories of good guys versus bad guys, whether Indians and Englishmen or Muslims and Christians, are always easily seduced by the sounds of gunfire. Kill the Commies! Kill the Cong! Bury Saddam! seem like easy solutions. The enemies change but the tune remains.

———•———

FIVE

Fredericton

The villages of Chéticamp and Grand Étang are close to the water, which makes complete sense, because we earn our living in the ocean more than not. But not that long ago, about a hundred years ago, Grand Étang was largely situated behind the first set of mountains. Which doesn't make any sense, because this is a long way from the land you could cultivate and from the ocean.

When I was about sixteen, I asked my mom why the village used to be back behind the mountains, and her answer was: To hide from the English. I can read my mom's emotions like she can read mine; they're fine-tuned, she's so expressive. In her answer there was anxiety; she was connected to that.

Her grandfather would have heard firsthand stories of the Deportation. My mom would have heard the story from someone who had heard from people who had lived it as children. And I thought, this was real. This really happened to us.

Roland Doucet

Fredericton is a town rather than a city, and to my eyes, one of the most charming in all of Canada. It is set down next to the Saint John River like a doll set, with a sharp escarpment on one side and comfortable farming country on the other. Constable would have painted the river and the town resting gracefully beside it if he had passed this way, and it would have looked as fetching as any place in East Anglia. In his stead, a long line of local painters have depicted the town glowing in the colours of all the seasons. The best known is probably Goodridge Roberts, who painted in the 1940s and '50s. The disembowelling hand of modernity seems to have been stilled here.

Set high up near the crest of the escarpment is King's College (now the University of New Brunswick), built with the warm, reddish bricks and the clean lines that favour all New England colleges. The founders of these colleges believed the ideal physical form of a university was a herd of reformed Protestant churches. There are even simple white steeples on many of the buildings.

Directly below the university are tree-lined residential streets with gabled houses that turn almost imperceptibly into the principal commercial streets. The main street runs along the riverfront between Theatre New Brunswick at one end and a nineteenth-century military barracks at the other. A grassy park next to the river has been kept for walkers, joggers, and cyclists. In the summer, rowers go winging over the surface of the Saint John.

In its imperial years, Englishness was exported town by

town in boxes sent across the planet from India to Australia to Canada. Fredericton was one of those boxes.

If the Acadian deportation marks the beginning of the British Empire, the growth of Fredericton marks its rising tide. With the passage of years Fredericton has become Canadian but for years was so overladen with Anglicanism and the sentiment of Empire that Lord Beaverbrook kept it in his hip pocket as a kind of talisman against all that was evil in the world, such as labour unions, American slang and "things common." The definition of "things common" was not specific but included all things he deemed inappropriate. Today, this would include the Irving brothers, who live in Saint John and presently own most of the province, and the McCain brothers, who live in Woodstock and own the remainder.

Fredericton was built during that long flush of English imperialism which justified itself by the notion that British culture was simply better than anything else. Hence, it was morally preferable that native cultures be displaced or modified to be in tune with the superior culture. In the beginning, the moral ascendance of things British was a rather shaky concept. It was more like good old-fashioned pirate plunder. Better that we have the gold than the Spanish have the gold. Better that the land be controlled by the English than the Hindus, Maori, Beothuk, or whomever. But pirates are unsettling no matter what uniform they are wearing and are best left alone. And young

Englishmen were mostly left alone to collect world geography like so many flashy buttons.

Colonel Lawrence ordered the Deportation without the approval of the British Colonial Office. Today this is sometimes cited as an indication of Lawrence's dyspeptic and authoritarian nature. Perhaps he was dyspeptic and authoritarian. But he was also doing what British bureaucrat-soldiers thousands of miles away from home did over and over again: he acted without waiting for anyone's blessing. Seventy-five years later, Colonel By pursued his immense Rideau Canal project with the same kind of single-minded determination as Lawrence showed during the Deportation.

Both colonels died without glory at home. Lawrence because he was a scapegoat for a decision the Colonial Office would never publicly admit had even been made but would de facto approve, without taking responsibility. Colonel By was disgraced more deeply because his transgressions involved money. (He had spent more money than the British Parliament had approved to build the canal.) Both actions were typical of the timidity of the Colonial Office and the vigour of the men pushing the boundaries of empire on their home office's behalf. Young John Winslow of Boston expresses the essential notion of "England *über alles*" in his diary without even the varnish of a British military career intruding on his thinking. "We are now hatching the noble and great project of banishing the French neutrals from the province."

The Acadians weren't hostile but they weren't English speaking. Nor were they Protestant. Worst of all, they weren't politically subservient. The Acadians weren't about to put on kilts or turbans and march off to fight for the English Crown. And it was this refusal that was too much for Colonels Lawrence, Monckton, and Winslow to swallow. (In 1968, two hundred years later, the descendants of the United Empire Loyalists would still be singing "God Save the King" and feeling offended that young Acadians at the Université de Moncton refused to sing along.) Different religions, different languages, even different skin colours could be tolerated in the nascent empire as long as the loyalties were clear. The one thing there wasn't room for was neutrality. Military neutrality was too close to out-right independence. Military loyalty had to be to Britain. The Highland Scots, the Gurkhas of Nepal, the Sikhs of India were what Britain wanted: tough, loyal, and appreci-ated servants of the Empire.

The Acadian exile marks the beginning of geopolitics – politics based on the attempt to enforce a planetary agenda. Ironically, the Acadians were more a part of the emerging world than the English in Fredericton were. For, in spite of all their travails, the Acadians were not feudal. The Acadians' independent, democratic ethic presaged the modern era, which arrived powerfully a generation later with the American and French revolutions. Their egalitar-ianism was so foreign to the sensibilities of Governors Cornwallis and Lawrence that neither could imagine any way of coping with them except by getting rid of them as quickly as possible. It simply wasn't within Cornwallis's imaginative reach to conceive it possible for a community to have foreign policies different from the king's. Nor should this be surprising; Governor Cornwallis was a peer of the realm. The existence of a peerage was predicated on obedient subjects. From this perspective, it isn't hard to see why the Acadians were regarded as a noxious weed.

Independent Acadian communities were burnt to the ground and the people deported, but the Acadian independence of mind survived. Some Acadian families, such as the Robichauds and d'Entremonts, even arranged to be delivered by the British authorities to towns in Massachusetts where they had business and social connections. Both families prospered and returned to Nova Scotia and New Brunswick as Loyalists, the Robichauds to continue successful business and family enterprises there. One of the Robichauds' descendants became premier of New Brunswick.

But the town of Fredericton had its feet firmly in the *ancien régime*. Fredericton was all about feudal loyalty. Even for Acadians today, Fredericton has the feeling of being on the other side of a divide. It has about it the vestiges of a world in which Acadie has never belonged.

SIX

English-English and French-French

I don't think historians exaggerate the consequences of the
Deportation, because [the Acadians] were so linked to their
land and communities.

You can read this in the petitions that they addressed to
the different colonial governments of New England, New
Jersey, Pennsylvania. It was the same thing when it was tried
to integrate them in France. They petitioned the king of
France at Versailles, saying they were sorry but they were not
French any more, they were Acadians and they were not used
to this ancien régime – a term that the French themselves
would adopt a generation later, leading up to their revolution
in 1789.

Maurice Basque, Director of Acadian Studies, Université de Moncton

In my grandfather's village, people would distinguish the European French from the Québecois by calling them French-French. By that measure, my mother was English-English. Acadie was a mystery that I was left to unravel for myself, but English-English was an open book. Above the blackboard at my school in St. John's there was a map of the world showing the British Empire in pink. Because of the northern distortion of the Mercator projection Canada appeared as a vast pink balloon under which hung the insignificant green pannier of the United States. I think this is the reason why to this day I cannot take the United States as seriously as I should. In my mind, it is a vestigial place where the beautiful and the bizarre co-exist in a weird but frivolous extraterrestrial tango. How could it be any other way, when with a little bit of foresight the Americans could have remained snugly within the great fold of the British Empire?

The British Empire was simpler to comprehend because it was linked together by the culture of the heroic public-school boy. It was a culture that, at the age of ten, I was part of every morning as I tied my school tie, pulled on my grey flannels and awaited my turn to swagger around as a bigger and better version of what I already was. In this world, India and Pakistan were the great pink fist and finger of Asia. I have never been to India and probably never will go, but Paul Scott's *The Jewel in the Crown* took me further into the same colonial world that the simple adventures of G.H. Henty and Kipling had started me on as a child. It is a world where the pebble thrown in the water is British and the ripples are ones that I have felt in my own soul. For me, the long agony of Scott's young Indian hero, caught and then ground down between the cultures of India and England, is far more resonant than, for instance, King Lear's rage against the misfortunes of old age and the ingratitude of children.

On the map, the Pacific was Australia and New Zealand, which were huge and splendid with mountains and prairies and verdant harbours. Like Canada, only with swimming instead of hockey.

The African continent was dominated by the roar of the lion and by the pink squares of Nigeria, Kenya, Tanganyika, the Rhodesias, and South Africa. The other countries of that enormous continent were just green spaces at the edges of the pink. Later, some of the complexities of Africa were impressed on me during my high-school years by such books as *Cry, the Beloved Country* by Alan Paton and Chinua Achebe's *Arrow of God*. I slowly began to understand that novels such as these could be more than just good stories for schoolboys. In the hands of a great soul, a novel could push back the frontiers of human sensibility just as science advances our knowledge of the physical plane.

The rest of the world I knew little about. I understood there was something wrong with South America because it had no pink. I was told that Russia was Churchill's "enigma wrapped in a conundrum." China existed for me principally as the caricature from Gilbert and Sullivan musicals. *Voilà*, that was the English-English world. The entire globe wrapped in a neat package, with the centre in a little island off Europe, and at its heart, the great city of London. I was born into this world as surely as I was born into Grand Étang and the comings and goings of Acadie.

My mother was a Londoner, born and bred in that vast and venerable metropolis that has been inventing and rein-venting itself since Roman times. The names of famous people and places came as easily to her as did the Cape Breton fishing seasons did to my father. St. Paul's Cathedral, Drury Lane, Westminster Abbey, Piccadilly Circus, the plays of Shakespeare – they were all part and parcel of my mother's youth.

In 1943, the year my mother and father met, London had the feel of a life raft floating in a wild and violent sea. A world war at Britain's doors, the Thames estuary was jammed with the drab outlines of camouflaged ships waiting their turn to unload or depart, the streets were crowded with uni-formed men and women. Summer evenings were split with the whine of air-raid sirens, the days with the usual hustle of the city.

Katherine Emma Oliver and Fernand Joseph Doucet must have seemed exotic to each other. My mother speak-ing in the clear, fluty tones of a London grammar-school girl; my father with the accents of Acadie. But it could not have just been the accents that they found exotic, it must also have been the places they were from. London was home to symphony orchestras, theatres, pubs, double-decker buses, the underground, policemen with bell-shaped hats, all of which must have been amazing to my father, who had been brought up in a village where the principal institutions were a small, wooden church, a schoolhouse, and the fishing wharves.

My mother and father don't talk about their romantic lives, at least not to their children, but there are clues in the few black-and-white snapshots that have survived. My father is blond haired and incredibly thin in his dark-blue air force uniform. He is six foot and barely weighs 150 pounds. My mother, photographed in a nurse's uniform, has shoulder-length raven hair and that peaches-and-cream complexion English girls are famous for. Both together and apart, they look rather racy.

War-time romances were often ragged, and my parents' was no different. They met at a dance given at the London hospital where my mother worked. After the dance, my father offered to walk my mother to the tube station. She accepted, but as they arrived it closed for the night and they were obliged to walk across a dark park in search of a taxi near the American officers' YMCA. It began to rain, and there weren't any taxis. Forty-five minutes later, they arrived at my grandmother's house, both drenched. My grandmother refused to let her daughter's soaking wet friend leave in the dark. She gave him some dry clothes, hung up the wet ones, and he stayed the night in the spare room.

A day or so later, an English pilot phoned Katherine Oliver and said he could not make it to a play that they had planned to see together. His leave had been cancelled; she should take someone else. So she phoned the young Canadian who had stayed at her house. She had an extra ticket for a play, did he want to go?

He did.

Fernand Joseph Doucet must have realized quickly that being the only child of a man who wore a suit to work and a *chapeau melon* on his head was a little different than being the eighth of ten farm children. In the Doucet family, people did not sit around a polished mahogany table and pay attention to their manner of holding a knife and fork. The dining-room table at the Doucets was made of rough pine and often had sixteen people around it for Sunday dinner. My father likes to recall his first graduation – from the corner of the table to a place along the side. In London, peasant life had long been wallpapered over. Shit was not necessarily shit, and Catholics were Irish.

All people develop a dance of manners around each other. The Acadian dance tends to be a loud, boisterous, *sauve-qui-peut*/may-the-best-man-or-woman-win attitude to conversation. I love it, but everyone has to be singing the same tune for it to work, and I am sure Joe and Elsie Oliver found this boy from Canada a little on the rowdy side for polite company. Just as I am sure my father must have been bemused by his future in-laws' tight rituals and social circumlocutions. Nor do I doubt that there was a sense of relief among the elder Olivers when, a few months later, the tide of war swept their daughter's Canadian beau off to Italy.

Fathers are always mysterious to their sons. There is an opaqueness that comes between them which is a necessary separation for the survival of the son; the influence of the father is so enormous, the son must seek some distance to become himself. My father has a lot of medals from the war. I've never inquired about them. Nor has he ever offered to explain, but the few stories that he did tell have had an influence out of all proportion to their telling. His squadron landed near Naples and was stuck there on the beach-head for three months. The Allies were unable to push the Germans back, and the battle had settled into the bloody attack and counter-attack reminiscent of the trenches of the First World War. A seaside town was caught within the Allied beach-head, and Dad took to walking there when he wasn't occupied with planes. On one walk, he met an Italian schoolteacher. They fell into a very difficult, broken conversation with much use of hands. The next day, Dad went back into the town with a Cape Breton friend and for a small sum they hired the teacher to teach them Italian in a formal way with books and exercises. I have this image of the three of them, the two Canadian boys and the Italian teacher crouched over their books in an empty café while the arsenal of war rumbled around them. It struck me as a little boy as an eminently sane and sensible thing to do, and it made me very proud of him.

The other story comes from some months later and concerns some chickens. All soldiers' food is canned, dried and monotonous, and theirs was no different. There was nothing fresh and yet they were travelling through some of the best farming country in the world. One day, three guys from my father's squadron showed up at his campsite with some stolen hens and bottles of wine. They were Toronto boys and knew my father and his friends were from the country. They figured the country boys would know how to prepare and cook the chickens. My father looked at the dead hens and then turned to his friends and asked each in turn what his father was. Each one of the boys said, "a farmer."

There was a long silence; the hens had been stolen from an Italian farmer. Then my father took the dead birds and said, "We'll cook them this time, but not again."

This idyllic image of my father at war is only partial, I know. He also helped to kill people. He was an air-force armourer, which meant he and his crew mates transported and installed the bombs and ammunition the planes carried. He kept the machinery of war going in a vivid, violent way. But my image of my father at war is not of bombs and destruction or medals, it's of him standing up to his fellow soldiers on a hot day, in an open field, for an Italian farmer he would never meet.

When Fernand Joseph Doucet got back to London, he wasted no time in looking up his English girlfriend, Katherine Oliver. And the romance rekindled. My favourite picture of my mother and father is the portrait taken on their wedding day. The cliché of every wedding photograph is accurate: they are both radiant. No other word will do. My father has a great, ear-to-ear, shit-kicking smile. He is scarcely out of his teens and yet, perhaps because of the uniform, he looks quite grown up. My mother looks both demure and like a film star with her dark hair, fine skin, and the small hat with a little veil she's wearing.

The Second World War was such a vivid and important part of my parents' life that it has become part of mine, as if I lived through it too. When I first read *The Siren Years*, Charles Ritchie's memoirs of London during the blitz, it felt familiar to me – the dense smoke over St. Paul's, the evening gloom of the blackout, the sound of massed planes and the whistling fall of bombs. Those scenes all echoed on long after in my parent's lives, and resonated in the lives of their children.

I know Fredericton not just as a pretty little city. I know it from the inside out, because there is a part of me that is unequivocally English-English. When I listen to the choir of King's College Chapel at Christmas time, I hear not just a magnificent choir but also the song of my own youth and the schoolboy choir that I once sang in. The poems of Wordsworth, the plays of Shakespeare, the novels of Hardy are also my poems, plays, and novels. I have internalized them as millions of English people have done before me. The competition of the rugby pitch and the exhilaration of the rowing scull have always been close to my heart. I have inherited these things as surely as I have inherited Joe Oliver's long Norman face.

Is it possible to have two identities? In Ottawa, I have been called a false francophone to distinguish me from a real francophone. I think this is always the way it is with people who have a strong sense of belonging to two different cultures. It isn't a comfortable place to be, but it is a creative one. People normally take their language and nationality for granted as part of their daily existence, just as a fish takes the water for granted. But if you have two strong identities, you are constantly, vividly aware that nations and languages are nothing more than social constructs. People invent them. The inventions and their applications vary.

My father handled his dual identity by building invisible boxes. One box was labelled Acadian and French-speaking, and the other was labelled modern and English-speaking. The Acadian box was cherished but private. He allowed himself to open it only when he was talking to relatives and childhood friends. Shutting up half of yourself is hard and ultimately, I believe, it creates a kind of cultural malaise. I see a strong parallel between my father's childhood and that of an Indian boy who grows up on an isolated reservation where he learns one language, one way of looking at and being in the world, and then as a young adult moves to the world outside the reservation where a different language is spoken

and there are many subtle but essential differences in the
rules of social engagement.

For my father the modern world was so enormous, so
imposing, it demanded he conform to its language and its
rules. The only other solution was to go back to the reservation where unlearning the "modern" world would be
harder than the initial lessons of conformity. Building sep-
arate interior boxes, one labelled Acadian or Indian, the
other modern and Canadian, is often the only way of sur-
viving this clash of languages and cultures. When I see a
brown face begging on the streets, all I can ever think of is
how hard it has been for the Indian people; how much more
they have had to suffer.

For me, it was different. I wasn't born on the reservation. I never "left" for the modern world. I never had to
learn English: it came with my mother's voice. For me, the
issue of identity came the other way around. I was born in
the modern world but grew up always feeling at the edges
of my existence that there was another place to which I
also belonged. For the longest time, these things were all
very confused in my mind. Each summer I followed my
grandfather's footsteps. I learned French. And all the
time, I was very certain that I would never live in Grand
Étang. I would never be a farmer like grandfather. I would
be a modern person. The Acadian part of me would always
belong to the past; this was the way it had to be. Then, as
I grew into my twenties, the conviction that I did not

want this to happen began to take shape in me. I did not want to build these private, internal boxes. I wanted to find bridges between the two worlds that would allow me to be true to my grandfather's world as well as a useful citizen in the modern. I did not want to be exiled from one or the other.

———•———

SEVEN

Wars, Heroes, and Identity

They don't consider the Mi'kmaq as "the other." They con-sider them as neighbours. This means that the relationship between those who are developing the Acadian villages in the seventeenth century and the Mi'kmaq and Malecite peoples is much a better relationship than anywhere else on the conti-nent, as far as I am concerned. For example – and I think this is very important – when Charles La Tour's Mi'kmaq wife died, he sent two of his daughters to Europe. One of them ended up singing in Vienna before the Holy Roman Emperor. It was recognized that he had married her according to Catholic rites; it was recognized that marrying Mi'kmaq, for those who were founding Acadie, was not something to be looked down upon in the seventeenth century. That's a very different attitude from New England or Québec.

Naomi Griffiths, Professor Emeritus, History, Carleton University

Graveyards are the principal product of war. Wars produce them the way a car factory produces cars. In Fredericton, there is an old graveyard in the centre of the city in which Mi'kmaq and Acadians are buried. It was once the graveyard of Pointe-Ste-Anne, an Acadian village burnt in 1759 by Lieutenant Hazen, who was continuing the work of the Deportation. To this day, New Brunswick Acadians petition the government for the right to raise a monument here to those who died or were exiled from Pointe-Ste-Anne, as has been done at Grand-Pré in Nova Scotia.

For Darrell Paul of the Union of New Brunswick Indians, it is a Mi'kmaq graveyard, and he cites as proof that the Malecites, who are part of the Mi'kmaq confederacy, made their first request in 1779 to the new British authorities for the ground. They were denied.

The Acadian position is that the Malecite chief at the time was an Acadian named Aubin and that in 1933, when two skeletons were exhumed from the site, it was concluded they were two young Acadian women killed at the time of Lieutenant Hazen's attack. The two skeletons were kept in the Canadian Museum of Civilization in Hull, and three analyses were done to determine whether they were the remains of Indians or Acadians. None of the analysis was conclusive, but it seemed more likely that they were Indian. In 1996, the museum returned the skeletons to the Malecites, who buried them at Pointe-Ste-Anne.

As well as Mi'kmaq and Acadians, United Empire
Loyalists are also buried in the old graveyard. These Loyalist
graves date from their first, terrible winter in Fredericton
after the American Revolutionary War, or the War of
Independence – depending on which side of the 1775 fence
you're sitting on.

One thing is crystal clear: the old graveyard by the
river is not like other graveyards, because it is a physical
reminder that the land on which Fredericton stands was
taken by force; that injustice is part of the Canadian scene.
This is not the kind of thing Canadians like to remember.
We have developed a national specialty for papering over
the past with the appearance of consensus, and we pass off
any difficulties that might have occurred as temporary dis-
ruptions in normal broadcasting. This is one of the reasons
Canadian children so often report that Canadian history is
boring and that the histories of other countries are more
interesting. It's not true.

Americans have long perfected a triumphant vision of
their history, which sweeps in one straight line from the
Mayflower and the pilgrim fathers of New England, through
General Washington and the Revolutionary War, through
Abraham Lincoln and the Civil War, through the conquest
of the West under the 7th Cavalry to Martin Luther King
and the second fight for liberty. It is very easy for young
Americans to get a fix on their history because America has
created a vast patriotism buttressed by great icons who sym-
bolize huge swaths of the American experience.

Made in the U.S.A. is made in the U.S.A., not just in products but in triumphant rock 'n' roll, triumphant films, triumphant flags, triumphant economics, triumphant armies, and triumphant democracy. To be a winner is to be American. Both the Americans and the French have developed an extraordinarily deft way of iconizing their nation's history, then putting it on a convenient shelf to be taken out at important moments when it's necessary to remember and summarize their national voyage.

Canadian history is much more difficult to grasp because it has been harder to line up the good guys on one side and the bad guys on the other. Was René Levésque a good guy or bad guy? It depends on who you talk to. For me, it is very clear he was a good guy. Others regard him differently. Was Louis Riel a good guy? For me, it is very clear. He was. Others regard him differently.

By American definition English Loyalists were the traitors, the bad guys. Benedict Arnold is an American synonym for traitor. In Canada, they have taken on a different colour. They are remembered as pioneers and by many as patriots. It is difficult for Americans to comprehend the existence of political refugees from their brand of patriotism, be they English Loyalists, Vietnam draft-dodgers or modern American Indian leaders such as Leonard Peltier. In Canada, the colour of patriotism has always been complex.

Louis Riel bestrides Canadian history as a giant caution to all those who would like to cherish nationalist, religious, or racist chauvinism at the expense of the human community. He was a great spirit, treated abysmally both in his time and by history. His defeat and execution was a loss that destroyed the possibility of a different, more humane, more interesting Canada; a Canada in which people of aboriginal descent would have been central to the country's development instead of marginalized by it. It is one of the great and lasting tragedies of our history that he was executed instead of being made the first member of Parliament for the new province of Manitoba. Louis Riel was demonized as a Métis French Catholic rebel instead of treated for what he was, a legitimate leader of a people with profound and important claims on the land and its governance.

A sense of ironic self-deprecation is Canada's most human and attractive national characteristic and likely the reason we produce so many wonderful comedians. Our least endearing trait is a gluttonous sanctimoniousness that I find hard to take. The way Canadian journalists treated Ben Johnson at the Seoul Olympics was not pleasant and is just one example of this. After the initial charges of drug abuse, not one voice was raised on his behalf, not one journalist gave him the benefit of the doubt or defended him. Yet Ben Johnson was a victim as much as a perpetrator of his own downfall: a victim of all those couch potatoes who want to win medals via their television sets; a victim of coaches who pushed him unrelentingly to win at all costs. The sanctimonious outrage against him the instant he failed his drug check was far more repugnant than the sin of a young man giving in to the pressure to win at all costs. My sympathies were with him then and remain.

There have been a few uncomplicated Canadian heroes, people we can love and admire without the slightest reservation. I met one of the few when I was driving up Kelly's Mountain, above the Bras D'Or Lake in Cape Breton, one miserable, grey day with a steady, foggy drizzle coming down. Out of the gloom emerged this lonely figure running at the edge of the road. We slowed down to watch him run, bent into the wind, his shirt soaked, his hair matted, his eyes focussed on the road ahead. He was running in a strange way, leaning to one side and pitching his leg around, his shoulders jumping sharply with each stride. As he went by I realized with the force of a body blow, the young man only had one leg. The other was made of metal.

Later, I learned his name was Terry Fox and that he was running to raise money for cancer research. But if he had never become famous, I would still remember that moment. I have always regretted that I didn't follow my instinct and ask the driver to stop so that I could run along with him for a while. When I think of unequivocal heroes, he is one that comes to mind. He took on a desperate illness and battled it for all of us, with the only winner being humanity, the only loser himself. That is a struggle worthy of heroes.

John Winslow's cheery statement, "We are now hatching the noble and great project of banishing the French neutrals from the province," could be seen as heroic to someone of American descent and differently if you are of

Acadian descent; or you can be more realistic about the limitations of the naked ape. This desire of young Winslow to pursue a war doesn't seem strange or particularly repugnant to me. On the day of my sixteenth birthday, I joined the Canadian naval reserve. If I'd been born earlier I would have followed the drums of the Second World War just as quickly as my father did. And if Canada had had the misfortune to join in the Vietnam War, I would have gone in a flash. By the time I was eighteen, some of my friends were so keen to get into a uniform and go to Vietnam that they crossed the border to sign on with the American military.

It seems foolish now. Vietnam had nothing to do with Canada. The people of Southeast Asia were as geographically and culturally remote from us as it is possible to be on this planet, but Canadian boys dressed in plaid shirts and bearing hockey sticks blithely signed up to go to Vietnam, just as earlier generations had for the Korean and two world wars.

After a war has run its ulcerous cycle, books are written and films made, and the reasons for the fighting are rationalized this way and that. There was this treaty to honour. The enemy was part of the "evil empire." There were atrocities to stop or to avenge. But these reasons are the reasons of old men. Wars are never fought by old men. They are fought by young men, often still in their teens, and for young men the permission to be violent in the name of patriotism has an enormous visceral attraction. It takes very little to inflame a young man with the music of marching feet and the lure of a uniform no matter whether the year is 1755 or 1945 or 1965 or 2005. When Alexander the Great marched off with his friends towards the East to conquer the world he would be distinguished by his success, not his motivation. The freedom of war has always been seductive to young men.

The simple, raw adventure of journeying to distant countries is a wonderful inducement all by itself. Just as the Second World War gave my father the chance to leave the rustic shores of Cape Breton for the romance of Europe, the Vietnam War offered me the mysterious East and the chance to play with real machine guns, tanks, and helicopters. For a young man who is just coming into his independence, war is a narcotic whisper. It takes very little persuasion for the enemy to become the bad guy and for the human being in your sights to melt into a caricature Commie, Gook, Serb, Catholic, Arab, Boche. Death and dismemberment are just unpleasant, improbable side effects. In the main, war will be the time of one's life. It's easy for boys to think this way because most boys are surrounded by the culture of war, not just in films and comic books, but in their own family histories.

My family is no different. In my mother's wedding photograph, my father wears the uniform of the Royal Canadian Air Force. On the wall, there is a painting of my Grandfather Oliver, wearing the impressive, full dress of the Household Cavalry. On my Grandmother Oliver's bureau, there was a more sober photograph of Joe Oliver outside a hospital tent in France with some friends. They are wearing formless, colourless wool uniforms. One man wears a bandage, stained with blood, around his head, another has crutches, another has his feet swathed in bandages. Grandfather is the only one without a visible bandage. They do not look like happy campers. Grandfather Oliver survived four years in the trenches of the First World War. Afterwards, its shadow hung about his large, athletic frame like the mysterious albatross of the Ancient Mariner. I could not help but want to join the military, it was as natural as breathing.

What I was defending would have been of slight consequence. I would have joined the Russian army if I was a young Russian, the American if I was American, the Vietnamese if I was Vietnamese. It was only many years later that I began to realize the emptiness of my gesture; how little it had to do with the Acadian side of my house and how much it had to do with heedlessly following a path laid down for young men for millennia, going back to the time of migrant tribes washing across the planet looking for places and people to conquer.

How naïve those early Acadians were. How could they have ever thought that they could avoid the age-old call to arms?

EIGHT

---•---

Jerusalem

Sumer is icumen in,
Lhude sing, cuccu!
Groweth sed, and bloweth med
And springth the wude nu.

Author unknown, first recorded by John Fornset, a monk at Reading
Abbey, 1250

For the summer holidays, Canadian parents who can afford it send their kids to camp, where they can splash around by a lake and forget there is such a monstrous thing as school. My parents could have done this easily enough. They had the financial resources, but it was in neither of their backgrounds to do this. It was not an English-English custom to send children off to summer camp. In England, for the summer holidays, you sent the children to stay with relatives in the country. In

67

her childhood, my mother was sent to Aunt Dolly in Great Munden, the little village where her father had been born and her grandfather had been headmaster of the school. My father was Acadian, and Acadian boys, as soon as they were strong enough, helped their fathers on the farm or in the fishery. I don't think it ever occurred to either of my parents that their eldest son should go anywhere in the summer but to his grandparents'.

It wasn't as easy as going to camp. Aunt Dolly and Great Munden were several thousand miles across the ocean. Grandfather Doucet and Grand Étang were not quite as far, but a good deal more remote, there being no plane to take me there. This did not dissuade my parents. When I was eleven, they put me on a large, four-engine prop plane and told the stewardess that my grandparents would pick me up at Heathrow. I was not sure I would recognize them, but my parents assured the stewardess that they would recognize me. This seemed entirely reasonable to me and I set out with the same combination of trepidation and excitement that any youngster feels going off for his first time away from home.

In the 1950s, London was spanking clean, like an old penny that has been shined and shined. The debris and violent emotions of war had been brushed away, and people were quietly getting on with their lives. Hammersmith, where my grandparents lived, was in the heart of the city, only a few minutes by tube from Westminster Abbey and the Houses of Parliament, but Hammersmith itself was not much different from a country village. There were few cars. A little boy and his grandmother could jaywalk casually across the high street, which my grandmother did habitually, convinced that the rules of road were for lesser mortals. She was too busy. The cars could wait. This rather arrogant approach seems to have been imprinted on me; to this day, I have trouble using crosswalks and waiting for the green light.

In my childhood, the high street in Hammersmith was not surrounded as it is now by shoulder-high steel railings to stop unwary pedestrians from falling into the unrelenting stream of cars, trucks, and buses. You could stroll to St. Paul's church, which sat on a green island in the centre of the square exactly as if was the centrepiece of a country village. There were no pedestrian tunnels under the road to get people safely to the church, and no elevated expressways sending high-speed traffic over the life of the square. The high street itself was a wide boulevard circling the elegant church, its shops providing a confection of delight – the sweet shop, the tea shop, the pub, the greengrocers. The morning food market was jammed comfortably into an alley just off the square, the narrow street running with water and filled with the pungent smells of fresh fish, brine, pickles, the fruits of the countryside, and the raucous greetings of stall owners, its essence unchanged since Shakespeare's time. In the square proper, by the entrance to the underground, paper boys sold the morning papers, Gypsies offered shoe shines, and the shimmer of adventure lurked below where the tube rumbled in an eternal shuffle back and forth from the centre of city.

The high street in Hammersmith sticks in my mind like the first taste of candy floss at the circus. I had never seen anything like it before. It remains with me today as the civil heartbeat of urban civilization, comfort, and adventure.

In 1957, London was both a great city and a series of villages with mementos of the greater world placed here and there like so many wondrously ornamented elephants. The Tower of London, Albert Hall, Westminster Abbey, St. Paul's Cathedral and the Thames swishing by Hammersmith on its way to the wide world beyond. Even a young boy from Canada, scarcely aware of himself, could not help but feel the weight of history around the great city's neck.

As the summer unfolded, my grandmother toured me through London's shrines, the dome of St. Paul's, Poet's Corner in Westminster Abbey (which seemed rather shabby to me. I remember thinking that if I were a poet, this would not be a good end). The Crown Jewels at Tower of London, which I remember looked like hats with gems stuck in them. I was more impressed with the Tower itself and especially the armoury, where the armour worn by the Black Prince was on display. To my astonishment, he was about my height and stature.

My memories of that summer are all immediate and vivid, like flashes in the dark. One of the wonders of childhood is that you take people and places as you find them.

The canvas of your life is not large enough to make com-
parisons or see horizons beyond the immediate. It is only
now, peering back at that boy that I can fit him and the
events around him into some slightly larger pattern.

My grandparents lived a life that was entirely mysterious to me. I was used to a house and a neighbourhood
crowded with children and activity. In St. John's, on a
Saturday morning, I could walk out of the front door,
whistle once and have enough friends for a softball
team, whistle twice and have two sides. Their house was not
on a street like that. I never met any children on it. The
house itself was eerily quiet and well ordered. The sound of
a radio was always coming from some room, but never the
one I was in. My grandparents seemed to spend very little
time together. My grandfather would be gone to work
before I woke. On weekends, he would take me to a football game or down to the Embankment for a lemonade and
some chips. We would watch the rowing skiffs go by, and
he explained to me about the great Oxford and Cambridge
race which we went to see, I think. I was small and the
crowds were large.

Grandmother never came with us. All the places that
Grandfather liked, she did not. She did not like boating, it
was boring. She did not like football, it was boring. For the
seaside, Grandfather was partial to Brighton and Grandmother liked Eastbourne. Grandfather came from a big,
village family. Grandmother was an only child. Grandfather
had a tricky heart and liked to walk and talk slowly.

Grandmother liked to talk and walk fast. Grandfather liked a beer in the pub. Grandmother liked tea in a tea shop. Grandmother went to church on Sunday. Grandfather met her afterwards.

There was a reserve, a dignified, English properness about Grandfather, which he wore like a curtain. He was always carefully attired and measured in his speech. The only time I saw him without a jacket and tie was when he went to Great Munden in Hertfordshire to stay with his sister, Dolly. Then the tie would come off, and he would roll up his sleeves and chop wood, prune trees, work in the garden. He seemed to smile more in Great Munden than in London, but he never stayed longer than the weekend, then he was back to the city, sometimes leaving his grandson with his sister.

Great Munden is a picturesque village like the ones that you see celebrated in calendars that show a dreamy country place awash in flowers and soft colours, forever quaint and forever beautiful. At one end of the village was a tiny church dating back to the Norman conquest. It resembled a large stone hut, its walls so thick I am sure it will endure for another nine hundred years. Inside, it has the feeling of a cave, with windows that let in enter slivers of light. My great-grandparents, grandfather, Aunt Dolly, uncles, cousins rest in its shady graveyard close by the front door. It is a beautiful place in the way of places that are steeped in a keen sense of themselves. If poets have not lolled about its graveyard composing idylls and elegies then they should have.

Not far from the church was the school where Aunt Dolly taught. In the middle of the village was the only shop. Across the street from the shop was a blacksmith's shed and a sprinkling of the more imposing houses of the village. From here, there was a tranquil view of farmland that curved over gently rolling land.

Aunt Dolly had been a school mistress, as the term went, for more years than anyone cared to remember. She had never married and, according to my grandmother, was a bitter old spinster, the love of her life having abandoned her for another. She didn't seem bitter to me. She had a wealth of affection for her numerous grand-nieces and grand-nephews who were shuttled off to spend the "hols" with Aunt Dolly, just as her nephews and nieces had once been.

Aunt Dolly lived in medieval squalor. The Black Prince in 1342 would not have felt uncomfortable dropping in for a beer and a little fried bread at Dolly's. Her cottage had no indoor plumbing and no electricity. No electricity meant no stove, no electric lights, no television, no refrigerator, no hot water on tap, and so on. It was a wonderful place to be a child because there were none of the rules that the amenities of modern life impose. Aunt Dolly didn't give a fig for what people thought or how clean you were or weren't. Her nieces and nephews woke up when they woke up, went to sleep when they were tired, and played with what came to hand.

I have no trouble imagining Tolkien's hobbit hole because I have lived in one. The hedge at the edge of the lane in front of Aunt Dolly's house was as thick and as intimidating as a forest. You could not see in and you could not see out. The lane itself was so narrow and sunken from centuries of use that it was easy to imagine hobbits and elves travelling on it. The cottage was romantic and beautiful, buried in the heart of a great tangle of apple trees and raspberry canes and hollyhocks and scratching chickens. It seemed to have grown out of the earth rather than to have been built on it.

Inside the cottage, it was always dark with only ribbons of light coming through the small leaded windows. There were two rooms on the ground floor and three bedrooms on the second. The cottage was heated by one small fireplace, and on that fireplace Aunt Dolly did all her cooking and heated all her water. I would go to sleep on a feather mattress with the window open, and sometimes the swallows that nested under the eaves would come swooping into the room, so that it was hard to know if I was sleeping outside or inside. Aunt Dolly's only concession to modernity was a battery-operated radio on which she listened to her favourite program, *The Archers*.

Aunt Dolly was a rebel. I think that's why children loved her. She had built an impregnable fortress out of her orchard and cottage. When her young beau chose another she should have gone away, my grandmother liked to say, and in a way she did. She went away without moving. No one could get into her territory who wasn't invited. It was dangerous. She had a dog that would tear the leg off the postman if he opened the gate. But once inside the gate, her kingdom was magical. There were eggs to be gathered. Trees to climb. Raspberries to pick. Tangled bushes to build forts in. Walks down to the open fields.

It was there we watched the hunters charge after benighted foxes, some of which had the good sense to go to ground in Aunt Dolly's orchard, leaving the hunters snorting at her tangled boundary.

Aunt Dolly would stand before them, long and lean and blue eyed, smiling and chatting. The hunters would grumble. The hounds would howl and prowl the scent line. Her big Labrador would stand snarling, ready to make mincemeat of anything that crossed the line, ready to toss the smaller dogs like they would have liked to toss the fox. Aunt Dolly enjoyed the hunters' discomfort. When it was over, she would say to me, "Nothing like a good hunt spoiled." Her day had been made.

She told me that Charles Lamb, the poet, lived nearby, and one day, we went down to visit him. He was a stone bust, stuck beneath a tree. How she laughed at my astonished expression, for I had assumed he was a living person. In the evening, we would play cards, and the loser would always have to read a verse of poetry.

Every now and then, her brothers would invade and

spend the weekend in a hurricane of cleaning and painting and mucking up the garden, the woodshed and chicken run; then they would go, and the cottage would sink back into its comfortable chaos.

She must have been able to afford more. She had been a teacher for many years and on her retirement received Maundy money from the Queen. (Maundy money is special money minted for the Queen to give out at Easter to select people. I think it used to be a feudal charity, but with the passage of time it has simply become honorific. It was a big moment in the village when Dolly bought a new hat and went down to Westminster to get her Maundy money.) But perhaps Aunt Dolly really couldn't afford more. A spinster who owned her own acreage and her own house was unusual. Most women weren't able to achieve this much. Ordinary people in England in the first half of this century did not have the kind of material wealth we think of as normal today. My relatives, at any rate, didn't have it. In many ways my grandparents had accumulated even less than Dolly. They rented their house in Hammersmith and didn't own a car; the extent of their possessions was nothing more than a few sticks of furniture and the clothes that they wore about the city.

My grandmother was not fond of her husband's sister. Nor was Dolly fond of my grandmother, but they put up with each other for his sake. Genetics are always a curious muddle. My grandfather Oliver and I look alike. I have inherited his size and steadiness. There is an Englishness about me that is clear as a bell, but also I have inherited the Acadian quickness, and that combination has stood me in good stead all my life.

My Aunt Dolly died at a great age, well into her nineties. Before she passed away, an antique dealer bought the entire contents of her house for fifty pounds and stripped it before anyone in the family could say boo. With the dealer went her father's desk, pens, mementos, and all her leather-bound books. A developer bought the cottage. It was on the county historical list and could not be torn down. While doing renovations, the developer accidentally knocked down a wall and the cottage was officially declared an unsafe structure. The developer was then allowed to tear it down and replace it with a modern bungalow. According to my cousin Kevin, this is standard behaviour in England for someone who wants land that has an embarrassing old building on it.

There are always two journeys. One is the physical trip, crossing oceans, doing things, and meeting people. The other is the journey that is remembered. The second is the more important, the one that illuminates the rest of your life.

When my parents asked me how the summer had been, I opened my suitcase and took out the little black-and-white photos I had taken and showed the gifts that I had bought. They were from Harrods, which in my memory was a great London store laden with toy castles and battlefields of little lead soldiers all perfectly painted. I told my friends about the hunters in red jackets milling about on horses and swearing, the hounds howling, and my aunt looking like a Druid queen, her grey hair flying in the wind, her eyes like blue steel, her mouth laughing.

But if you asked me today how was that summer when I visited my English grandparents, I would tell you it felt to me as if I had seen everything in the world that was worth seeing. I had done it all and would never have to travel anywhere again. There was no point in going further; I had seen Jerusalem and all its myriad connections. I had imbibed a sense of how the English world fitted together in the give and take of life under the Union Jack.

Anthony Trollope's novels of county life and county families seem quite modern to me, quite close to the bone. I understand perfectly how that small English county society – bright, populous, and above all eccentric – spawned the generations of soldiers, artists, and travellers who were obliged to leave for great cities and foreign countries because their own world was too small to hold them. I can feel it in the history of my own family. No one but Dolly stayed in Great Munden. There was no room in the village. All the others migrated to London, to the north, to the colonies to become musicians, businessmen, social workers, soldiers, filling in the cracks of society.

I can feel the passionate characters of Jane Austen and Emily Brontë in the history of the Olivers, although Jane Austen never created a character of the power, beauty, intelligence, and blind pig-headedness of Aunt Dolly, or a hero such as Joe Oliver, who fought more bloody battles than is ever worth fighting and felt the emptiness of defeat in his older years. He carried England on his broad shoulders as surely as any poet buried at Westminster. When I read Siegfried Sassoon's "Memoirs of a Fox-Hunting Man," it is always Grandfather Oliver that I think of. He had Sassoon's simplicity, limpidity, and courage, without the jangling sensibility.

Elizabeth Bennet in Austen's *Pride and Prejudice* is my grandmother, Elsie Oliver, a beautiful woman with a beautiful daughter who woke up one morning and realized with a great shock that she had not married Mr. Darcy, from which neither she nor her marriage ever fully recovered. This is, I think, a phenomenon peculiarly English. An astonishing number of women in England are still raised to be witty and engaging consorts of Mr. Darcy. The problem is, there is always a terrible shortage of very rich, dynamic, handsome, and morally impeccable Mr. Darcys.

The English imaginary landscape – C. S. Lewis's Narnia, and that of Tolkien in *Lord of the Rings* – make perfect sense to me both as imaginary creations and real places. Nor can I pick up an English poet, be it Shakespeare or Housman, and not see the landscape of London or Hertfordshire; or get in a rowing scull without thinking of sitting on the Thames Embankment with my grandfather, mystified by his enjoyment of watching little boats skim over the water. It takes very little for me to wrap these fond memories in Parry's soaring tune "Jerusalem," composed to celebrate that verdant isle where so many men and women have believed so unartfully in progress and decency.

But where did Acadie fit in, in this grand world of national accomplishment? Where were the little farms and fishing coves of Acadie? Was there a place? Or was I, as La Sagouine said, "with the Indians"?

Where was I?

---•---

Old Acadie

When we talk about societies that were created by Europeans, the Acadian society became the first one in America – even before the exile – that had this discourse, this political culture, that asked for special recognition within the British Empire, something the American revolutionaries only did twenty or thirty years after them. The Acadians were not really a society that had a very privileged link with the King of France or with the British Crown. Their most intimate link, the bond that they had, was to their land; their land that gave them enough food, that had enough cattle so that they could not only survive but have many commercial ties with New England.

When 1755 arrived, this just sort of blew up.

Maurice Basque, Director of Acadian Studies,
Université de Moncton

South of Fredericton, the Saint John River Valley begins to broaden, and the landscape here has the same lush feel as the Annapolis Valley in Nova Scotia. The river meanders, and there are islands where cattle graze. The gentle shores are populated by water birds and marsh grass. This is the land of old Acadie, which once spread in a great fan of farms around the rivers and marshes of the Bay of Fundy. Acadie was not based on a political vision, but on the land and the kind of life that arose from the land. In this way, the Acadians, like the Métis who settled in the West, were more aboriginal than European.

It was the landscape of Acadie with its dikes and low farmlands bordering the sea that Longfellow's Evangeline was going back to, not a country with political ambitions in the European sense; that is why the Deportation looms so large in the history of Acadie. It was not just the transfer of people from one place to another, it was the end of a culture that existed only in this part of the New World. When the war ended, many returned, but the majority, like my ances-tor Paul-Marie Doucet, would have been just children when the Deportation started. In the interval between 1755 and 1763 and the years that the slow return would take, they had become adults, but adults without a senior generation. Like many of the Indian nations, they had lost their elders. Longfellow gets this salient fact absolutely right in *Evangeline*. Evangeline's father is the first to die, and this is how it was in the exile: the old people went first. So when the new Acadie did begin to re-form in Atlantic Canada, it was not only removed from the landscape from which the original culture evolved, it was also separated from the generation of men and women who knew the most about it and had given it its greatest expression.

Paul-Marie Doucet is typical. He was eight when the Deportation started, and in his early thirties with three sons of his own when he moved to the shores of Cape Breton. What happened during the intervening years is not known. We know only that his wife, Felicity-Michel, was probably Mi'kmaq, and they likely came to Cape Breton from what is now northern New Brunswick. Perhaps from the fishing village now known as Caraquet. Thirty years is a long time to be without any fixed address, and by the 1780s, when Paul-Marie and Felicity-Michel arrived in Chéticamp, the Acadie of *Evangeline* was already drifting into legend.

Just as the first Canadian prime minister, Sir John A. Macdonald, deliberately did everything he could do to break up the cultural integrity of the Métis communities in western Canada, the British did what they could to prevent the Acadian communities from re-forming. Even after the colonial war ended in 1763, the Acadian deportation was not recognized by the British government as having ever happened. The original deportation orders were never revoked. The only recognition of the exile came in a negative way, in what Acadians such as Paul-Marie were not allowed to do: they were not permitted to buy back or resettle near their old farms around the Bay of Fundy. The only land permitted them was as far as possible from their original settlements at Port-Royal and Grand-Pré in the Annapolis Valley. Like the Mi'kmaq, they were pushed to the far edges of their old territory, to northern New Brunswick and Cape Breton Island.

The New Acadie had echoes of the old, especially in the language of seventeenth-century France and the curious mixture of local democracy, co-operative projects, and individual entrepreneurship and the love of place and community which would all continue to characterize the new Acadie. But the Deportation destroyed three of the original pillars of old Acadie – the elder generation, the marsh farms, and the long friendship with the Mi'kmaq people. The friendship with the Mi'kmaq had been essential to the independent character of old Acadie and was central to the Acadian ability to resist the political persuasions of France and Britain. Taking the oath to bear arms for the British Crown would have thrown the Acadians into war with the Mi'kmaq, who were bitterly opposed to the English. Again and again Acadian deputies used this argument as one of their excuses to refuse the English requests to bear arms.

After the exile, this long friendship disintegrated. Partly because disease and war reduced the aboriginal population from about 30,000 to a few thousand. As with the Acadians, the trauma of the long war and the annihilation of their people would plunge them into the grim business of daily survival. The loss of elders for an illiterate society is always a body blow. In a culture where governance, religion, history, traditions, songs, and stories are held only in the people's memories, the elders are the conductors, linking the past, the present, and the future. Without them, the society's spinal cord is ruptured.

The young Acadians who returned not only came to a different place, one which would require new ways of earning a living, but they also came without their elders to recall the past. Paul-Marie Doucet's three sons all remained in the new villages of Chéticamp and Grand Étang and raised families, from which my own family is descended, but Paul-Marie and Felicity-Michel did not stay. They drifted down the coast towards the Margaree valley. Where they ended their days is not known. The character and sensibilities of this couple are a mystery.

More than two centuries later, Acadians are beginning to be aware again of the long shared history between the Acadians and the Mi'kmaq. We are beginning to remember we have Mi'kmaq ancestors in our family trees. We are beginning to remember the acts of kindness the Mi'kmaq people showed us during the Deportation, evident because Mi'kmaq names often appear as godparents to Acadian children; and that there was a sharing of skills, trade goods, and homes from the earliest days of the Acadian colony. But in the long aftershock of the exile all of this was forgotten, and later, Acadians adopted the attitudes of the dominant society. The Mi'kmaq people were apart. They were the Indians. The Acadians were not connected to them. For some, racism developed. It was as if a great broom had swept through Acadian society, erasing not just the elders but our history.

The landscape south of Fredericton is still beautiful, still wonderfully bucolic with fields abuzz in the summer. In some places beside the tidal inlets, you can still see the vestiges of old Acadian dikes, but it is no longer Acadie and has not been for a very long time. The planet has revolved and the Acadians are no longer on this land. As I drive through, I find myself drifting off into interior views.

TEN

———•———

Conquistadors and Indians

Take up the White Man's burden –
Send forth the best ye breed –
Go, bind your sons to exile
To serve your captives need;
To wait, in heavy harness,
On fluttered folk and wild –
Your new-caught sullen peoples,
Half devil and half child.

"The White Man's Burden," Rudyard Kipling

One of the best aspects about travelling by car is the radio. Music is never quite the same any place else, not even in a concert hall. I have forgotten countless films and more books than I care to admit, but there are moments between me and the radio that will stick forever. I remember driving up to Ingonish, Cape Breton, and hearing Simon and Garfunkel singing "Mrs. Robinson." I can remember that moment as if it were yesterday instead of thirty years ago. Paul Simon and Art Garfunkel's voices had the robust, cynical purity of fallen angels. Outside the car, beyond the hearing of fallen angels, the deep summer billowed in emerald waves up the forested mountainside to the bluest skies. Below the winding, climbing road, the sea was silver.

As I drive towards the reunion I am listening to an interview with Mario Vargas Llosa, the Peruvian writer. He writes in Spanish but his English is flawless. In 1990, he ran for the presidency of Peru, and after being the front-runner for many months was defeated in the second round of voting by Alberto Fujimori.

If I were in the same room as Vargas Llosa, the crush of his fame and my own lack of it would be a wall between us. But with the radio, instead of a wall, there is just space. Vargas Llosa is sitting in a studio in London, England, the interviewer is sitting in a Toronto studio, and I am in my car somewhere between Fredericton and Moncton. We are like three points on a compass. Each of us equally important and equally unimportant.

Normally, I'm allergic to interviews with writers of all kinds. The first time I did a media tour to promote a book, the publicist eventually said in an exasperated way, "You're exhausting yourself because you're trying to answer every question seriously. Ignore the questions, just repeat the same thing at every stop." No doubt she was right, but since then I have had great difficulty listening to authors on tour. All I seem to be able to hear is the sell, but Vargas Llosa wins me over and I find myself comparing notes with the famous writer from Peru.

The book Vargas Llosa is selling is called *A Fish in the Water*. It is a memoir of his youth in Peru and, in alternating chapters, an account of the two years in which he campaigned for the presidency. Listening to him makes Peru seem quite close. His education, like mine, was a public one, but much richer. From an early age he was reading not just the classics of Spanish literature, but also English and French novels. As a teenager, he ordered Jean-Paul Sartre's famous magazine *Le Temps moderne* and read it in French. When he wasn't reading he was clashing with his friends in heated literary and political discussions. He not only knew who Albert Camus was when he got to Paris, he met him and they spoke briefly together in Spanish. (Camus's mother was Spanish.)

I find this all quite extraordinary. My preoccupations as a teenager were skiing, football, and girls, not necessarily in that order. If I considered myself advanced intellectually, it was because I took the time to read the actual books on our English course instead of the Coles Notes. My idea of the universe was about as complex as a maple tree turning red in autumn and the idea of writing as a career was as strange to me as becoming a ballet dancer. Some people in foreign countries did these things, but not Canadians. In my last year of high school, when Vargas Llosa was writing and mounting his first play, my friends and I were stealing chickens from the federal experimental farm and depositing them in our school principal's garden. We thought this was an excellent way to spend a Saturday night. A political statement for us was checked shirts, jeans, long hair, and Kodiak boots. This was supposed to signal to the older generation that unlike them, we were in touch with ourselves, the common man, and maple trees. We felt ourselves to be the finest fellows in the finest of countries. If we had a political philosophy, it was simply that the rest of the world was not enough like Canada.

Mario Vargas Llosa speaks very eloquently about the various authors that he has read and their effect on him. I listen, amazed at his erudition. He seems to have absorbed the entire Western literary canon, much of it in its original language. He is both a writer and a professor of modern literature. I have no idea how to rank the various authors that I have read over the years in any order of importance. Each seems important to me but in different, not comparable, ways.

I remember reading Margaret Atwood's first novel *The Edible Woman* in a laundromat on Spadina Avenue in Toronto and thinking to myself, Oh, so this is what Canadian literature is supposed to sound like. *The Edible*

Woman had the ineffable stamp of Canada and the sixties upon it. It became a kind of fulcrum in my mind, with Canadian authors divided into B.E. (Before Edible) and A.E. (After Edible). And as with A.D. and B.C., everything B.E. was old, and everything A.E. was modern or modernizing.

Scum of the Earth by Arthur Koestler made a huge impression on me. It is Koestler's account of how the French government efficiently locked up all left-wing antifascists inside enormous barbed-wire camps at the start of the Second World War. The "scum of the earth" were the idealists, the intellectuals, the republicans, the communists, the remnants of the international brigade who had fought against Franco. Albert Einstein's brother appears and disappears among the other prisoners. And when France capitulated, the keys to the camps and all the prisoners are handed over to the Nazis as a kind of hors d'oeuvre to the Holocaust.

What a devastating read. It was like watching someone raise an axe over the head of a helpless animal; each day, each week, each month, the axe descends a fraction closer to the outstretched neck. Koestler, a journalist and survivor of the Spanish Civil War, was caught in the net along with the rest, and his memoir recounts his many desperate efforts to escape the axe. I read it while I was living in France and could relate personally to his journeys from one government office to another as he tried to get some government official to give him an identity card. He often seems close to getting his papers, but never quite close enough – there is always another piece of paper that he needs. This is the way the French government has worked since the revolution. The royal *lettre de cachet* sending a citizen to the Bastille has become the republican *carte d'identité*. *Plus ça change, plus c'est la même chose.*

If I could wave a magic wand, I would see on school reading lists in every country books that expose not just the nobility of the nation, but the underbelly of the national condition. Books that record nothing but the long scream of mindless, Yugoslavian pain. Maybe then citizens of all countries would be less inclined to beat their chests in virtuous amazement at the mindless savagery of others.

For the radio interviewer I could go on recounting books that I have read in a relentless genealogy of authors I feel are related to me by virtue of my having turned the pages that they have written. But to what purpose? How do you classify one as more important than another? How does Koestler fit on the weigh scales with Atwood?

There were no books in my grandfather's house, none at all, not even a family bible. I don't remember missing them. Our days were full. They started before six. I would go downstairs as soon as the first rays of summer sun began to slide through the bedroom window. Grandfather would already have a fire going in the kitchen stove and a pot cooking on its surface. Breakfast was a grand meal: porridge, bacon and eggs, toast and jam, tea and more tea and more toast and jam. We ate it quietly, taking our time, and then walked out to the barn, our stomachs comfortably full, to begin the morning milking.

There was no room in the day for reading, for reading is a secondhand experience. The pages of a book give you the world through the prism of someone else's days, but on a small farm, you have no time for anything but your own sunrises and sunsets. It is these summer days I recall more often than the pages of any book, no matter how much it has impressed me.

How are you going to be in the world?

How you answer that question is the compass you use to navigate the uncharted years. And I answered that question with my grandfather's example. He never told me that I should be this way or that way. He told me stories as we split wood in the evening for the kitchen stove. I learned skills: how to use an axe; drive horses; cut hay. He was not a tall man. He was lean and fine-boned and tremendously strong. And I learned from him the many differences between strength and power. Strength was all about having the energy, intelligence, and patience to accomplish a multitude of necessary tasks: boxing an open spring to protect it from the muddy feet of cattle; repairing fences; training a horse with steady, directing affection. Strength was never about power over other people, it was about having a generous spirit. Grandfather always had time for conversation, neighbours, and friends. He had very little use for power. He did not say what people should do. He kept his own farm so impeccably that soon after the hay was cut, the fields looked like putting greens. But how someone else farmed was how they farmed. I watched him and learned not to judge. I learned about honesty and how to treat people with great courtesy. I learned that sometimes you cannot be as generous as you might wish. You cannot let a smoker sleep in your barn. I learned that stories are important; that they are the way we make our souls visible to others.

During the Depression, grandfather hired a taxi so that people from the distant parts of the village could vote. He voted Liberal but hired the taxi for anyone who needed it, because he thought it was more important to vote than who you voted for. At grandfather's, I never read a book, but I learned all the important things that I have needed in life. The things that you cannot learn from books. The things that form the skeleton of all my days.

I have spent much of the rest of my life trying to explain to myself in words what I understood then instinctively. I would learn to say things like "business profits are not earned by taking business from a rival"; that real profit – the kind that sustains life for a long, long time – is formed by creating value where none existed before. As the Acadians did when they diked the marshlands. As engineers do when they invent new machines. But these are just words I use to externalize what I feel deeply in my heart. That nations and communities become successful, important, worthy when they learn to build on each other's strengths, not beat each other in destructive competition.

———•———

When I listened to Mario Vargas Llosa, I did so in two minds. We do not share the same world view. I do not believe that the price of success, that modernity must be paid for by the extinguishment of others' hope. I think this is fundamentally wrong, and it is a divide between us that cannot be crossed because this is a belief he does not share. In this regard, I do not feel either modern or European. I feel only the heartbeat of my Mi'kmaq grandmothers, and it is them I honour.

My literary ear remains impressed with his formidable erudition. He is a scholar as well as a writer. He segues elegantly from modern literature to the Spanish conquest of Peru without missing a beat. He describes the conquest of the Inca empire not so much in terms of military victory but as the clash of two incompatible systems in which one was obliged to collapse and the other to conquer. For Vargas Llosa, the deciding factor was not the Spaniards arriving with horses and guns, initially appearing to the Incas to be some mysterious God-like chimera of animal and man, but the Western culture of individualism. When the Inca and his two sons were murdered by the conquistadors, the vast Inca empire collapsed because it had no other way of governing itself. The Inca warriors and Inca generals were not able to organize the defence of their empire without the Inca or one of his sons to replace him. The notion of obeying had been instilled in them by centuries of social deference, from the highest to the lowest levels of society. Killing the Inca was like stunning the central nerve in a primitive life form where all the other cells are attached to that one central spot; the queen been of a hive.

The Inca empire, this enormous social organization which fed and clothed millions of people, which occupied the entire spine of the Andean Cordillera, with towns and villages flung over thousands of miles all connected via an amazing highway system, should have been able to drown a few miserable white men in an ocean of angry Quechuan warriors. Instead, it unravelled as harmlessly as a soft ball of llama wool and its bewildered armies were slaughtered like so many cattle in an abattoir. Thus began the centuries of oppression that would reduce twenty million people to six million. The fabulous wealth of Peru would be mined from by the descendants of the conquerors in centuries of ugly evisceration. The French-French have an expression to indicate unrealistic wealth. It is, *C'est pas le Pérou!* It's not Peru.

Vargas Llosa honestly pronounces what many others don't have the nerve to say in these times of political correctness: that the American aboriginal culture and the Western culture are simply not compatible. One or the other is obliged to go. He describes the aboriginal as archaic, the European as modern. History is mute testimony that he must be right because we have seen this happen everywhere. Unless the native population was so enormous that it was beyond being suppressed in a direct way, as was the case with China and India, the story the world over is depressingly similar. The Europeans who arrived in Australia called it *terra nullis*, the empty land. The aboriginal inhabitants were not counted as human. This wasn't extreme. The North and South American experiences are not much different. Sometimes, a small accommodation was made, for example setting up reserves for natives in North America. The American general Philip Sheridan described U.S. reservations as "usually a worthless piece of land surrounded by swindlers."

When it comes to aboriginal peoples, I don't believe that Vargas Llosa's book learning serves him well. He is simply repeating the conventional received wisdom that has justified the European treatment of the New World and its peoples from the beginning. The behaviour of the Europeans, whether they were conquistadors, the American 7th Calvary, or the North-West Mounted Police, is best explained by the way the Europeans treated each other, which was to do battle until one side won. It is not very sophisticated. The biggest guy on the block wins.

Louis Riel made the distinction between brute force and the resolution of differences through civil discourse when he said

> You must understand, there were two nations,
> one large and powerful,
> one smaller and less powerful,
> two unequal nations,
> but no less equal in rights.

These words ring in my mind as both true and uncompromisingly modern. They express a world view that does not require the simple subjugation of one culture by another, instead it requires mutual respect and a willingness to share the fruits of the earth and the governance of society. There has never been a willingness to do this by any European civilization.

The thing that exiled my ancestors, burnt our villages, and is burning the Amazon today is the primitive notion that the world is an endless jungle, in which only the most competitive beasts survive. This is a simple way of stating the political and economic world view of modern corporations and modern nations, but the corpses of whole species, classes of people, and life systems bear witness to it. It is a notion that can be endlessly buttressed by references to the writings of the various schools of modern philosophers and economists and bankers on the importance of global competition, but in the end it comes down to the subjugation of people and the planet's resources by individuals or groups of individuals for the purpose of acquiring wealth. This is not the way that you create lasting wealth. You make wealth by creating value, by adding value, not by seizing it.

There is a difference. It is the difference between Edison and a buffalo hunter.

The present notion of world governance is much the same as it was at the time of the conquest of the Americas. Prosperity depends on being competitive; competition means winning; winning means beating the other guy as a football team beats another football team. The principal role of government is to assure the rules of engagement are respected, and to safeguard the gains of the winners. The new globalized economy is just another, more sophisticated, form of the plunder of the Inca empire. A few conquistadors are winning, and this time it is not just Peru but the entire planet which is losing.

This is not to say that before the conquest aboriginal people lived in some kind of Utopia where no one ever lost their temper and no one ever competed. In Canada, the Algonkian people had a long-standing animosity toward the Iroquois, just as the Cree did toward the Inuit in the north and the Sioux to the west, and so on across the continent. These aboriginal wars were ordered along linguistic and cultural lines. Warriors on all sides could be every bit as vicious as the conquistadors. Given a ready supply of guns by the British, the Iroquois almost wiped out the Huron. The great difference between the conquistadors and the aboriginal peoples, which Vargas Llosa doesn't understand, is that, internally, the Inca, the Cree and the Sioux, the Algonkians and Iroquois were organized on a co-operative model. The Europeans were not. This was the great divide between the Spanish, Dutch, English, French, and the New World peoples.

In the European model of society, there were no limits to competition. Competition didn't stop at the borders of England or New England or New Spain. The Europeans were not only extra-nationally competitive, they were intra-nationally competitive. In other words, when the Inca generals quietly laid down their arms, they were submitting to an ideology and a social construct that were entirely foreign to them. It was the same for northern leaders such as Sitting Bull and Big Bear. They laid down their arms and entered a world where the war would never be over because there was no limit to competition; where the concept of stewardship of the land and a sharing of resources was regarded as childish; where Chief Seattle's belief that "Man did not weave the web of life, he is merely a strand in it. Whatever he does to the web, he does to himself" was regarded as noble but foolish. In the European view, the planet and all of its life forms, including human, are there to be used to enrich life's winners; land must be competed for, mined, farmed down to the last county concession, to the last garden, to the last right of way, to the last oil well, to the last wild-rice marsh, to the last mineral deposit. No garden is too small for a fence. No resource so small it cannot be sold and resold. Centuries after the initial military conquest, land developers, lawyers, governments, and police forces continue the battle to exploit the New World's resources, even the water that flows over Indian lands.

Among aboriginal nations the notion that the Earth could be turned into a yard sale for the profit of a few was ridiculous. The real disaster for aboriginal people was not their military defeat, but European society's constant appropriation of their economy, vocabulary, land, animals, water, trees. The aboriginal world was relentlessly dismantled through education that denigrated aboriginal identity, through religious oppression and the physical destruction and appropriation of animals and ecosystems. The internally competitive system strikes out in every direction because it knows no boundaries. This is why people can starve to death in the richest nations on the planet while others enjoy a level of wealth that the Inca himself could not imagine. The Western model allows for only two kinds of citizens: winners and losers. You are successful or you are marginalized. You are either a conquistador or you are not.

This fundamental difference between the European-based constitutions, which form the legal skeleton of the modern global competitive system, and the aboriginal concept of society was described eloquently by Roger Jones, councillor and elder for the Shawanaga First Nation, near Sudbury, Ontario, when he said

> You read the Constitution, it doesn't talk about love.
> It doesn't talk about sharing. It doesn't talk about
>   kindness.
> It doesn't talk about honesty. It doesn't talk about
>   truth.

Where are the values of the people.
So really it doesn't have life.

The values of honesty, kindness, sharing, truth that
Roger Jones refers to are not about individual rights or
private-property safeguards, they are the community
values which form the basis for our responsibilities to
others and to our planet. They are the values which form
the glue that holds our governments, nations, and peoples
together; without them, no nation can hope to last long.
They are the values my grandfather taught me to honour,
not by what he said, but by how he conducted his life.
They are the values I cherish to this day and which form
the bedrock for what it means to me to be Acadian in the
modern world.

***

On the radio, Vargas Llosa comments in a bemused way that
you cannot simply dismiss the Inca civilisation because, after
all, it did feed, clothe, and house millions of people along
the entire spine of the South American Cordillera, an
accomplishment that modern nations cannot achieve. But
this fact does not change Vargas Llosa's view that they were
an archaic people, they weren't modern. There is nothing
surprising here. This view has been used to justify the
Europeans' theological, economic, and military suppression
of the conquered in the New World since the sixteenth

century. It began with the "great" debate over whether the aboriginal peoples had souls.

When my parents sent me to visit my English grandparents in 1957, London was still the centre of the conquistador world. The Inca empire paled in comparison to the English one, which spanned oceans as well as continents. The painting that my mother has of my grandfather in the dress uniform of the king's Household Cavalry is the portrait of a conqueror. He wears a steel breastplate and a tall metal helmet with a white horsehair plume. The serge coat is blood red. It is a uniform that European cavalry have worn in slightly varying forms for a millennium. With remarkably little change to the costume, my grandfather could be a sixteenth-century Spanish conquistador.

Everywhere I went in London that summer, I was reminded that this was a city of rulers. My grandfather took me to see Admiral Nelson on top of his column in Trafalgar Square and told me the famous story of his putting up a telescope to his blind eye so that he did not have to admit defeat. He looked splendid standing so high in the summer sun, with the pigeons circling around him.

At the British Museum, I saw the Elgin statues from the Parthenon. Forty years later, the magic of seeing their stone genius remains with me. I don't think anyone who sees these unequalled statues could ever be casual in their admiration for the civilisation of ancient Greece or not want to visit the place where they were carved. My grandmother took me to listen to Handel at St. Martin-in-the-Fields. It was the first time that I had ever heard choral music other than by a school choir, and I will never forget this either. If heaven has music it must be Handel's.

It seemed to me as a boy that the world was a huge, wonderful jug that had been tipped towards London, with all manner of things falling out over the city: composers, statues, paintings, poems, soldiers. Part of what was tipped from the jug was the displacement of New World aboriginal and Métis peoples. A scent of victory and confident accomplishment hung about every London park and street corner. My grandparents could not imagine there was anything on the planet that could quite equal an Englishman, and it was a great disappointment to them that their daughter chose not to marry one. If God was not an Englishman, there had been a mistake.

The radio interview ends with Vargas Llosa recalling a visit to Santa Maria de Nieva in the Amazon, a school for Indians run by nuns. His comments remind me that, in Canada, for a hundred years, we took Indian children away from their parents at age seven and sent them to residential schools run by religious orders who, just as in Santa Maria de Nieva, forbade them to speak their mother tongue. The children's concepts of spirituality and religion were discounted as trivial and superstitious. Their braided hair was cut, and they were indoctrinated in the "true religion." In Canada, the "true religion" was not always Catholic. It could also be "true" Presbyterian or "true" Anglican.

Vargas Llosa's account of Santa Maria de Nieva does not surprise me. What does is how consistent the European story of contact with New World nations has been. Centuries after the first meeting of European and Indian, the same ethnocentrism is still at play. Vargas Llosa is a sensitive, intelligent man and he acknowledges that the good nuns of Santa Maria are wasting their time because the Indian girls cannot be kept indefinitely at the mission school. He realizes that once they are indoctrinated they cannot go back to their former lives, but neither can they fit into European life except as cheap labourers or perhaps prostitutes. Vargas Llosa bemoans this, but simply as good intentions gone astray. He cannot conceive that the work of the nuns is a spiritual murder that springs from the same source as the military conquest.

I come from a different school and a different culture. I don't believe human beings have the right to play God with other people's cultures or spiritual lives. I don't believe we have the right to send neighbours to the wall as a price for our success. This is wrong. And if we do not learn this lesson, we will one day extinguish not just the archaic people but also the modern. In the end, the conquistadors will feel the bite of the bullets that they have fired at others. The bullets will turn on them. It is the logical end of the eternally competitive system that the Europeans invented. We will devour ourselves in a global swallowing that will leave nothing but the wrecks of communities, peoples, and eco-systems, all extinguished in the service of worldwide competition. For the European system can continue only if resources are infinite. For a long time the oceans and continents of our planet did seem to be limitless. There was always another Peru on the horizon. There were always more fish somewhere in the sea, more trees on the land, more people to be displaced. This has changed. We are now destroying the shores on which we are standing. The air we breathe.

The radio interview ends and I turn the radio off. The countryside is rich and bathed in warm evening sunlight. My dark thoughts clash with the soft, summer glow.

ELEVEN

———◆———

Moncton

This is the forest primeval. The murmuring pines and the
    hemlocks . . .
This is the forest primeval; but where are the hearts that
    beneath it
Leaped like the roe . . .?
Where is the thatch-roofed village, the home of Acadian
    farmers —
Men whose lives glided on like rivers that water the wood-
    lands,
Darkened by shadows of earth, but reflecting an image of
    heaven?

        Opening lines, *Evangeline*, by Henry Wadsworth Longfellow

It's said that the one thing above all else that characterized the old Acadians was their relationship with the land. It wasn't their culture or their religion or their language, it was their feeling for the land. Longfellow captures this sentiment in the first lines of *Evangeline*. But by the end of the poem, through the art of a great poet, it is Evangeline herself who comes to incarnate the story, the people, villages, and life of the old *Baie Française*.

Given the impoverishment of European peasants in the eighteenth century, Longfellow's bucolic garden images are not as fanciful as they first appear. The Acadians had founded a democratic, independent existence a hundred years before these ideas swept the European kings from their thrones. Nor was the old Acadie complicated by religious imperatives; Acadie housed Huguenots as well as Catholics. Acadie was unique, not in its ambitions and connections to biblical or royal imperatives, but in its disconnection from them.

When Colonel Lawrence ordered the villages of Acadie razed and the people shipped away, he expected that they would settle somewhere else, quickly disappearing into the steady stream of European people flowing across the ocean to populate the English-American colonies. But the Acadians were not immigrants from Europe. They had no Old World home to go back to; the only place that Acadie and Acadians existed in was the New World. They didn't want to start a new life in Boston or Virginia or Kentucky. Their lives were inextricably connected to the sweep of the sea around the Bay of Fundy; to the great fields behind the dikes; to the hills of hardwood trees, which curved up from the little villages along the shore. It was there they wanted to remain, not to settle elsewhere. The Acadians who were sent back to France foundered and were unable to adapt. They were used to governing themselves. They were not used to what they called the *ancien régime*. Attempts to resettle them failed.

The astonishing thing is that although Longfellow wrote *Evangeline* nearly a century after the Deportation, at a time when Acadie had been nothing but a memory for several generations, he touched on something absolutely fundamental to the Acadian experience – love of the land and love of community. If he hadn't, his poem would have long since become a literary curiosity instead of staying in print for more than a hundred years. The vigour of that vision is evident in that it appears not just in his own poem but re-appears in the works of twentieth-century Acadian historians such as Maurice Basque and poet Herménégilde Chiasson. Each treats the theme differently but none deny the power of it.

These words are from Herménégilde Chiasson, from a prose poem called "To Write":

First there was the land and then only a giant grave above which the murmur of distress and wandering could be heard.

It is the landscape of Maritime Canada which was printed on the Acadian heart, and nothing would dislodge it, not their physical removal from Acadie, not anger, not love. Those Acadians who did manage to return were obliged to settle so far from their old lands and from each other that it was assumed that they would never be able to reconstitute themselves into a people again. Like the Mi'kmaq, they had been put safely away on reservations.

The city of Moncton lies at the geographical divide between the old and the new Acadie. On the hillside where the Université de Moncton stands, you can feel the north wind from the Gulf of St. Lawrence, where Acadian fishing villages are now located, and on other days the south wind from the great estuaries of the Bay of Fundy, where the marshland villages of old Acadie once stood. Moncton is the capital of Acadie, though not in spirit, for every Acadian village is the capital in spirit; nor is it in the capital in name or governance, but if Acadie were to have a capital, it would be Moncton. It is here you find the professors, artists, publishers, theatres, and businesses of Acadie.

For an Acadian from away, going to Moncton has the significance of a pilgrimage. As the landscape begins to change from the rolling hills of the Saint John River Valley to the flat countryside of the Gulf shore, I can feel a certain tension. I want to be on my best Acadian behaviour, to make sure my French is as polished as possible. I don't want anyone to say, "Your French is good." The French are dazzling and subtle in the ways they can slight you over your accent and sentence construction. It is a universal affliction among francophones. The Parisians mock the Montréalais, the Québecois mock the New Brunswick Acadians, the Acadians from New Brunswick mock the Acadians from Nova Scotia, and the Acadians of Nova Scotia mock the Acadians from Wedgeport. The Acadians from Wedgeport mock the Acadians from away, which is everyone not from Wedgeport. This completes the circle. Mostly I ignore the jibes, and just remember what my grandfather said when he was learning English, "It doesn't matter if they laugh at you. Just speak. In the end, you will have two languages and they, one." He was right, but every time I open my mouth to speak in French, anxiety is always there in the background like a slight toothache. What category am I being slotted in?

A quarter of a million people are descending on New Brunswick for the Retrouvailles. Everyone from literary stars such as Antonine Maillet to great athletes like Jean Béliveau and women like the Doucet cousins from Montréal and Ottawa whom I met at the border. We are like salmon swimming up a river, each impelled by a force we scarcely understand.

Antonine Maillet is coming to the Retrouvailles as the uncrowned Queen of Acadie, chancellor of the Université de Moncton and the only Canadian ever to win the Prix Goncourt, speaker at all the principal events.

Where am I in this vast array? I wish I knew. There was one time when it looked as if I would also be a star in the

Acadian firmament. I have a picture somewhere, a glossy black-and-white photo of Antonine Maillet, Timothy Findley, and me. It's a publicity shot taken for the 1976 winter season at the National Arts Centre in Ottawa. All three of us had plays on at the NAC that season. Maillet and Findley were already established stars, and I was the new kid on the block.

Maillet went on to win the Prix Goncourt. Findley's books can be found in airport bookstalls around the globe. If I had to choose between the Goncourt and airport bookstalls everywhere, it would be a tough call. Sadly, I don't have that choice, although at the time the photo was taken, it seemed that my day in the sun was not far off. My first novel had been nominated for the *Books in Canada* First Novel Award, my first play was produced at the NAC, and my second book went through two editions and sold twenty thousand copies. It seemed that I was set. I'd won a Canada Council grant and took a year off from my day job to write my third book, which often is the one to make an author.

It never happened. *John Coe's War* became trapped in one of those obscure struggles which from time to time plague the launching of a book, and it was not reviewed until well after the season it was published. The reviews, when they finally came out, were fine, but it was too late. The books had all promenaded back from the bookstore shelves to the publisher's warehouse. They were stuck with a publisher's worst nightmare: thousands of books and nowhere to sell them. My career crashed.

Crashes, both physical and literary, are painful, but there can be advantages for a young writer. It gave me time to reflect, which is the staff of every writer's life. Why was I writing? What mattered? These questions were not trivial; they are at the heart of why any writer bothers to put words on a page. And I gradually learned that I wrote for only one reason: to play. Playing was the only thing that really mattered; for in play I could sometimes find intimations of my soul. With words, everything is possible. I learned that it was essential for my own happiness to understand the difference between success and fame. Success is composing a poem I am proud of for its own sake, and at the end of each day feeling that the gesture of my life has been as good as I can make it. Fame is something else. It may have something or nothing to do with success, but one thing is sure: measuring one by the other is a fool's game.

I've met Antonine Maillet on a number of occasions since that season at the NAC, and I have an interview scheduled with her at the Retrouvailles for a show on the reunion I'm putting together for the CBC. She can never quite remember who I am, so I always have to introduce myself carefully each time we meet. At the reunion, she will be the opening speaker at all the important events, preceding both Jean Chrétien and Boutros Boutros-Ghali. I will be at the back of the hall with the rest of the paparazzi.

I am an unreserved admirer of Maillet. I delight in the sound of La Sagouine's voice. She reminds me of my aunt Isabet. When she was very old, I visited her in the old folks home in Chéticamp. Even in her nineties, she was lively, complaining that the only problem with the place was the lack of men. I joked, "What would you do with a man anyway, Aunt Isabet?" Quick as a wink she replied, "Why, take him to bed. That's what men are for."

Moncton is the home of Viola Léger, the actor who has played La Sagouine all over the world. It's also the centre of the language divide, the watershed between French- and English-speaking New Brunswick. The city itself is neither French or English speaking, but both. The language frontiers curve through the city in invisible lines. Until you know where they lie, you're never sure which language should be spoken where. My father's generation solved this problem by never speaking French outside the confines of their village and family. It was kind of an unwritten rule among his generation that if there was an English-speaking person in the room, you spoke English. It was considered polite. I hated it when people immediately started speaking English when I was in the house, as if I had a big neon sign on my forehead that said, "Speak English."

The big struggle in the 1960s in Moncton was to bring French out from the private domain into the public spaces. The mayor of Moncton at the time was a man with the impeccable English name of Leonard Jones. He believed that French belonged on the reservation and told the young men and women of my generation in no uncertain terms where they could take their aspirations for the French language. He enjoyed considerable local support from unilingual anglophones and in the short term he crushed the student revolt at the university. But he was fighting against a national tide led by Pierre Elliott Trudeau, who had persuaded Canadians that it made sense for the federal government to operate in two languages where the population warranted it. The National Film Board made a documentary of the student strike, called *L'Acadie, l'Acadie?!?* Students occupied university buildings, sleeping in them, existing on high emotion, coffee, cigarettes, and the desire, often inchoate and poorly expressed, to be recognized as central to Acadie, to be more than just students. What they meant this was having a say in how the university was run, and being recognized in the city as Acadians with the right to speak French at meetings of the municipal council. The film of the student strike made visible for the first time to a wide audience the oppression that Acadians had long felt. There is an unforgettable scene in the film, when the students ask to be allowed to speak in their own language at their own City Hall and the mayor refuses them. It is difficult to watch and not feel the injustice of it as your own.

As a result of the strike, thirty students lost their places at the university and the department of sociology was closed down, but the students won the war. Mayor Jones proved himself embarrassingly small-minded on national television, lost an election, and drifted off into political obscurity.

Today, the two languages co-exist. Many businesses that rely on the telephone and computer have located in Moncton because national and international companies have realized it offers an educated, bilingual, and cheap wage pool. City Hall now keeps a bilingual public face. But the two languages co-exist uneasily. The problem is that even with the best of intentions, conversation can be held in only one language.

I've lost much of my 1960s naïveté. When I was a student at the Université de Montréal, I thought that everyone could be as bilingual and bicultural as Pierre Trudeau. It would just take a little work. I've learned that it isn't that simple, because a language is more than just a way of passing on information. It's a way of being in the world. It determines the kinds of newspapers and books you read and don't read, the films you see and don't see, the singers that you listen to and don't listen to, the friends that you have and don't have. Consequently, languages tend to be self-sealing. You are either inside one or you aren't, and in the real world there are few people who can cross these boundaries.

Although they are only a few kilometres apart, it isn't accidental that Shediac is unilingually French speaking and Sackville is unilingually English speaking. Nor is it accidental that the cantons of Switzerland operate along language lines. A person can speak many languages, but he can only live in one; that's why English bureaucrats in Ottawa ask "How's your French," and francophones are asked the same about their English, as if the other language is a pet they keep in the backyard and bring out to entertain visitors.

English is an eater of languages. When I first arrived in Moncton and began to order my meal in French, the young woman taking the order interrupted me politely but firmly, saying, "Sorry, but I don't speak French." I switched to English and asked the young woman where she was from, thinking she was from an English-speaking part of the province. Instead she said proudly, "Right here in Moncton." I learned that she had just graduated from Dalhousie University and wanted to become a police officer in Moncton. The dominance of the English language is such that a bright young woman can grow up in a city where close to one out of two people speaks French, and yet act as if the language didn't exist. When you consider this, it's easy to see why one side gets defensive and the other can't understand what the problem is.

At the Université de Moncton, which language is spoken is clear – it's French. Everywhere you go on the campus, you hear Acadian French. The anglophone world could be a million miles away. But drive a few kilometres southeast from Moncton to Sackville and it is difficult to believe that there is a French-speaking people less than an

ocean away. Sackville has the distinctive rural complete-
ness of a New England college town. Yet it is situated in the
heart of what once was old Acadie, almost within sight of
Fort Beauséjour and the old village of Beaubassin, from
which the Doucet family was deported.

If I turn north on leaving Moncton instead of southeast, in about a ten-minute drive, I'll come to Shediac,
where it is difficult to find a native English speaker. Shediac
is an Acadian fishing port with a great sweeping sand
beach and a long, narrow main street along the harbour. It
is here that Viola Léger, the actress who has been La
Sagouine on the stage for thirty years, teaches high school.
Shediac, Moncton, Sackville, these names resonate with
the complex history of Acadie. At the edge of Moncton,
you can still find the old dikes along the Petitcodiac. Many
of them have their water channels, or *aboiteaux*, still in
place. The size of these timbered channels, which stopped
the sea from passing through the dikes but allowed freshwater to drain off, is impressive. You can walk through
them scarcely bending your head.

On a summer day, the tops of the dikes make a wonderful path for a stroll. They rise about twelve feet above the
marshes and are about twenty feet across at their base. On
one side, the breeze from the bay gently bends the long
marsh grasses, and on the other the river rolls through the
tidal flats in a broad sweep to the sea. Here, the romance of
Evangeline and Gabriel can still be felt, because their story

is impregnated in the gentle landscape, in the dance of summer wildflowers and the noisy flight of shorebirds.

Despite the beauty of the landscape, I do not arrive in Moncton in a romantic mood. I'm tired and grouchy and tense. It's like arriving at a large convention where you're not sure you've got the right reservations.

TWELVE

Opening Day, Cap-Pelé

Frolicez-vous bien.

Mayor, Cap-Pelé

I drive from Moncton to Cap-Pelé by the Gulf shore. It is the first time that the size of the reunion hits me. The ocean highway is lined with Acadian flags. Some houses have been entirely wrapped in red, white, and blue banners. The Acadian star is everywhere. I feel like I am on a grand presidential pathway for some great dignitary. Everywhere the names of Acadian families are written and painted, on flags, on barns, on houses – Arseneault, Cormier, Chiasson. It is as if these names have swum in from the sea and beached themselves by the thousands on the shore. It is only about thirty kilometres from Moncton to Cap-Pelé, where the opening ceremonies will take place, but it is slow going because the entire highway has been turned into a village street, lined with parked cars and people. Music pours out of every building big enough to hold a stage. I can feel my heart beating faster than it should, as if there is some deadline that I have to meet and I am late. But I am on no particular schedule. The opening ceremonies are in the form of a "frolic" that starts at noon and will go into the night for as long as people want to party. There's no reason to feel in a rush, but like some poor demented salmon I am determined to get to Cap-Pelé for a rendezvous, the point of which escapes me.

The radio station from Shediac broadcasts news of the reunion as I inch towards Cap-Pelé. It suddenly hits me that the Cap-Pelé section of the highway is not the exception; that the flags and family reunions stretch along the entire Gulf shore of New Brunswick from Caraquet, near the Québec border, to Cap-Pelé, near the Nova Scotia border. A quarter of million people are celebrating. The bubble of happiness this vast image evokes is hard to convey. It is nothing but pure excitement that has set my heart pounding.

I park the car in a field overlooking the sea at Cap-Pelé. A soft breeze wafts in from the sea. It's a perfect day for a summer frolic. In the days of my grandfather, a frolic was something between a party and communal work. The most spectacular frolics were for barn building, but most were for smaller things, to card wool, cut wood, or finish a project before winter closed in. Afterwards there would be a party. The party was the way people were paid back for their work.

The stage is simple and quite beautiful. Its background flashes with little triangles that spin like sails in the breeze. The music is fine but it washes over the field from huge speakers in annihilating waves. When the bands are playing conversation is impossible. Fortunately, the music is interrupted by many speeches from many vice-presidents. The reunion has a vice-president in every Acadian village from Cap-Pelé to Louisiana. The president comes from Alberta. No one pays the speeches much attention. People wander about the field, stopping here and there to chat or just to feel the warm summer sun on their backs. Around the edge of the field there are food tents, picnic tables, and stalls with books and souvenirs for sale. A couple from France dance over the grass. Their hair is tinged with grey, but they seem the youngest people here. A clump of people wear crimson jackets, with "Cajuns/Texas" written across the back, and Texas Stetsons on their heads.

I'm supposed to be doing interviews for a radio show I'm working on, but the music is so loud, it drowns out the voices on my tape recorder. I try interviewing the Cajuns from Texas and learn that they first moved there from Louisiana in the 1930s when oil was discovered in Texas. They are descendants of the Acadians who were deported from Canada to France and who then journeyed back to the New World at the invitation of the King of Spain, who was looking for farmers for his colony at the mouth of the Mississippi.

The Acadians heard about the reunion in Texas and decided to come north to find out what the country that their ancestors had originally come from was like. They speak English with a broad drawl that I can hardly follow, but their French sounds like the French of my father. I ask a man with a weatherbeaten face how they have kept the language all these years. He just smiles and says, "In the family, mother to son, that is all. In Texas, we have no French in the schools."

I try several times to get their story down on tape, but each time the interview is interrupted by the music starting up again, so I put the recorder away and content myself with wandering about.

The day is clear and beautiful, but my mind is in a fog. I still haven't been able to figure out exactly how the reunion is going to work or how I will ever explain it to a radio audience. The Cap-Pelé Frolic is supposed to be the opening event of the reunion but it doesn't feel like it. There is little formality to it. I don't see anyone who looks vaguely mediagenic. If there are VIPs waiting to be interviewed, I can't find them. The frolic has the easy feel of an Indian powwow. Once I make this connection, suddenly everything seems okay. I don't have to be interviewing someone or doing something important. All I have to do is just be here.

I sit under a tree and pull out my guide book to the Retrouvailles. Even in two weeks, I couldn't attend more than a fraction of the events listed. There are just too many spread over too much geography. I'm going to have to focus. The question is where and how? As I flip through the book, I gradually understand that the reunion is subdivided into three general types of activity. There is the series of conferences and seminars at the university, which includes the Women's Summit. There will be over three hundred invited speakers at these conferences, everyone from the Parks Canada director at Grand-Pré to such heavy hitters as the Acadian nationalist Jean-Marie Nadeau. The second set of activities are the cultural events. These are concentrated in Moncton, but there are also events scattered along the entire Gulf shore, and they include everything from craft shows in school gyms to a professional musical, *Louis Mailloux*. The third set of activities are the family reunions, each one with its own events: picnics, dances, dinners.

In my imagination, the reunion has begun to resemble a series of Russian dolls, each nested inside the other, with the largest being the family reunions, the next-largest being the cultural events, and the smallest being the university conferences. I could spend all my time just at the family reunions or just at the cultural events or just at the university conferences. The two Doucet women that I met on the road will be attending just the Doucet family reunion in Richibucto. They are not bothering to go into Moncton to any of the cultural events. I decide to follow their example. Except for the giant show at Parlee Beach on August 15, I scratch all the cultural events. I'm left with the family reunions and the conferences at the university. I scratch out all the family reunions except for the one for the Doucet and Vautour families in Richibucto. I still won't be able to do everything because the family reunions overlap with the conferences, but with a few pen strokes I've at least given myself an itinerary which is possible to follow.

I'm not sure I'm doing the right thing. Some of the bigger family reunions, such as the Leblancs', will attract five or six thousand people, but unless I cut and paste myself through the next week I'm going to drive myself crazy trying to be everywhere.

It's difficult to tell how many people are at the Cap-Pelé Frolic because people are constantly coming and going. My guess is that at any one time there are three or four thousand, but given the number of official openings, I'm surprised anyone is here at all. Each family reunion has at least one official opening. The Women's Summit has an official opening. The university conference has an official opening. The cultural events have official openings. The more I ponder all these different official openings, the more it strikes me that it is very Acadian. One of the hallmarks of Acadie is democracy, and in a democracy everyone gets their say, everyone gets to be a president of something. So why not have lots of official opening ceremonies, with lots of official ribbon-cuttings?

During the exile, when the officials running the refugee camps in France tried to get the heads of the various families to make decisions on behalf of the group, invariably the response was that they could not; first they had to convene a meeting and discuss the matter. "This is what we are used to," was their explanation.

———•———

About three o'clock in the afternoon the attention of the crowd shifts suddenly from the stage towards the open sky. I turn with everyone else to see what is happening and notice several dots above a distant treeline. The dots grow larger, and I realize that they are skydivers moving rapidly towards us. There are three of them, dressed in the red, white, and blue colours of Acadie, and attached to their legs are large Acadian flags that wave violently in the wind. At first I think, How corny. Then, as the three figures become more distinct, I can see they are actually travelling very fast and are fighting hard against the wind to land at the fairgrounds.

The noise from the stage ceases and the crowd falls silent. You can hear a rustle in the grass. It is as if we have all drawn in our breath together, and I realize with a crack around my heart that I am not among strangers. I know them. I know their names. We are all related through time and travail. They are my relatives. They are called Chiasson, Leblanc, Poirier, Cormier, Boudreau, Richard. I think of their hard days working in Québec, in Louisiana, in Ontario, in Nova Scotia, in New Brunswick, of the journeys our ancestors endured. I think of my own aunts and uncles, my cousins, and the long road that took them to Cape Breton and then away again. And I am overcome with the weight of this long struggle to be ourselves without imposing on others, without fighting a war; to simply be. Suddenly, embarrassing tears come welling to my eyes, and brush them away, hoping that no one will notice.

One after another, the skydivers come tumbling down into the centre of our Frolic. And then I notice there are many other people around me with tears on their cheeks.

THIRTEEN

Grand Étang

Of this event [the exile], the poet Longfellow made much in Evangeline, *the story of a young girl separated from her lover in this vast act of dispossession. There is no question that this was a harsh measure, but Longfellow over-sentimentalized his tale, and peace came as a result instead of continuing war.*

Among the most prominent beneficiaries of this large-scale handout was the uncle of my great-great grandfather, Major Charles Dickson, a retired army officer who had led the exodus from Ireland, and had settled in Connecticut some year before. He had raised a company which played a leading part in the expedition to capture Acadia. For his share in the enterprise he was given three thousand acres of the richest land in the Minas Basin. He had no children. His heir was his brother's child, my great-great-grandfather, also named Charles. He had come to the province in 1760, as a boy of sixteen, and with his marriage and the birth of his large family we became Canadians.

Lovat Dickson, from his autobiography, *The Ante-Room*

The Acadian villages of Inverness County, Cape Breton, are situated on a small plateau overlooking the sea. The plateau is narrow, no more than two miles wide from the base of the mountains to the sea. It is beautiful country, but wild. There is a narrow canyon, which cannot be seen from the sea, that runs between the edge of the plateau and the mountains. It is a wrinkle in the landscape that the eye flows over. The tidal salt pond from which our village gets its name lies in this canyon. For many years my Uncle Gérard had a sawmill at the head of the tidal pond, where he would cut the logs that came down from the surrounding forest for the farmers and fishermen who needed cut lumber for buildings and fishing jetties.

I always loved the trip down into the valley. The road there was narrow and clung to the edge of the mountain. The valley was so deep, the views from the top were spectacular, the mountainside pitching down to the pond and the verdant forest below. There was a stillness within the valley that didn't seem natural after the constant wind on the plateau. In summer on the plateau, there was always a breeze from the sea, and in the autumn storms crashed around the village, rattling the windows with a primal force. But the wind blew harmlessly over the top of the valley, allowing the trees within its shelter to grow large and full. There was a succulent, almost sinful, quality to the valley, as if here the devils of existence had been kept at bay. It was the only place in the village where apple trees would grow, and most farmers like Grandfather kept a few trees there.

Above the pond, there was usually an osprey gliding in flat, broad circles. They have six-foot wingspans, and it was fearsome to see them floating above our heads. This eagle is the only one that prefers to hunt fish instead of mammals, and the pond was a perfect hunting ground, being shallow, clean, and restocked with fish by every tide. As we descended the mountainside, there would sometimes be a whoosh of sound as one passed overhead. The power and speed of their passage sent shivers through me. If you were driving, you had to be careful or the horse would shy dangerously at the movement of the great bird, upsetting the wagon in a tangle of broken equipment.

When he was younger, Grandfather had operated the mill but had passed it on to Uncle Gérard, who also did some logging on land that he owned on the mountainside. Grandfather's days of hurrying to work were over. He no longer drove into the valley with a pair of horses and a dozen jobs to be done at once. Now, there was an easy ambulatory ride to our descent. He would stop and rest the mare whenever she got tired. We would talk. Just about anything could impede our progress: a rabbit bounding across the road or a spruce tree that looked as if it had some particularly inviting gum. This we would pare off from the bark with a pocket knife and then all that could be heard for a long while was the sound of chewing. Spruce gum is tasty but sticky. If I live to be old, I would like to be old like Grandfather, with a horse and cart and my grandson or -daughter with me. I do not want wealth or convenience.

When there were raspberries ripening in the cutover woodlots, that would be our destination, but if Uncle Gérard was at the mill, we would stop there and talk. Perhaps share a mug of sweet tea. Perhaps load some sawdust in the cart for barn bedding. Perhaps not. I would be allowed to play in the sawdust mound as if it were warm snow. I thought it was a wonderful thing that I had an uncle who owned a sawmill. I realize now that as these things are measured it was a very small mill, taking only a few men to operate. Often, it was more a community mill as Uncle Gérard would make special arrangements with men who needed logs sawn but did not have much money. Part would be paid in labour. Part would be paid in something that would be useful to Gérard. I think that this was how the dikes must have been constructed and operated in old Acadie. They belonged to one farmer in particular, but they were built and operated under complicated arrangements between kin and neighbours. No doubt, there were occasional disagreements.

Sometimes, Grandfather would pick out a few fence posts and we would load them on the wagon. He always kept a stack of posts in the wood yard, because repairing fences was a perpetual task. There was a complicated sharing arrangement of who was responsible for the common fences between our long, thin farms. This was the source of some grievance for my grandfather because he was meticulous about his section, but his neighbours were not. Occasionally Grandfather would drop a new fence post beside a rotting one as a signal to his neighbour to fix his share of the fence. More often than not, he would just fix it himself, for he wanted his farm to be just right and it offended him when his neighbours cared less for the details than he. He never said anything straight out to his neighbours; in a small village, you must get on with people. You depend on them and they on you. In the matter of fence posts, an unwritten account was kept. If Grandfather fixed too many of Arthur's posts, at some point Grandfather would ask him to help with a chore that required two men, and Arthur, who was a better carpenter than farmer, would come willingly. There would be no charge for this labour. In this way, Grandfather was paid for the new fence posts.

I did not understand how these things worked in a formal way because no one told me, but I learned them nonetheless. In the city I did not understand how people worked together. My father's work was at an office, and what he did there, how he treated people and they him, was a mystery to me. But it wasn't this way in the village. I watched Grandfather and learned.

After stopping at the mill, we would clip-clop down the narrow, gravel road to a forest clearing that was part of Grandfather's woodlot. There, we would pick the raspberries that grew in profusion among the old logs, all the time with an eye out for bears, which also liked raspberries.

One time, in pursuit of some particularly succulent berries, I almost bumped into a large black bear sitting on his haunches as if at the dinner table, calm as could be, scooping up great pawfuls of berries. He looked up at me, his mouth smeared red with juice. He did not understand that this patch of land was owned by the Doucet family, nor was he interested in leaving his berries because of a small intruder. I retreated, my heart beating fast, half frightened, half grumpy at the bear for hogging the best patch.

Even in my childhood, there was little around the salt pond after which the village was named but the dark, green forest and a few old clearings, but there used to be homesteads. The forest had grown over these old places, and occasionally you would come across the stone outline of an old basement or some tall garden flowers standing guard in a comical, lonely way for a building long gone. These faded prints of human passage gave a ghostly character to the little valley, and I would sometimes find myself standing quietly listening for the sound of voices in the stillness.

One day, I asked Grandfather why people had moved from the valley and he said it was because there wasn't enough land. There was not enough space for a cow, and the mountainside was too steep to cultivate. I understood immediately what he meant, because a cow without sufficient space to wander quickly grows miserable. It wasn't a convenient place for fishermen, either, as it was a long walk to the harbour and you couldn't float a boat properly in the salt pond. At low tide, every boat would have been canted on its side. So why would anyone want to live in the valley? It never occurred to me to ask.

I'm not sure how or when I learned why people had moved into the valley. My cousin Roland can. He asked his mother, who said, "Well, to hide from the English, of course." Her reply is graven in his memory because it was the first time he realized that the Deportation had really happened, that it wasn't some remote incident that had happened to other people. It had happened to us, here in Canada. The memory of it was still written indelibly in his mother because her grandfather, who was a hundred when he died, was told stories of the exile by people who had lived it as children. Two centuries is not that long in the memories of people.

When I first heard the story of the Acadian exile, I did what all children do with something that upsets them which they don't understand. I buried it. The Deportation meant that a redcoat, my English grandfather, had forced at gunpoint my Acadian grandfather to abandon his farm. This was not plausible. It was not something my English grandfather would do. Nor did it seem possible my Acadian grandfather would ever have abandoned his farm. So I buried the story. And, as often happens, it came back when I was older. It came back coated with the lustre of my early memories.

FOURTEEN

Warren Perrin

In Moncton, small clusters of film crews promenade, looking for photo ops. Street performers playing the fiddle and the accordion for spare change from the passing crowd are circled by cameras balanced like electronic logs on the shoulders of young men. It is impressive. In New Brunswick, there has never been anything like it. The New Brunswick *Telegraph Journal*, which usually covers Acadian news in summary stories written by stringers, has page after page of photographs splashed from the front page to the back. The Moncton *Times-Transcript* and the Fredericton *Daily Gleaner* are much the same. Acadian nationalists such as Jean-Marie Nadeau can't quite believe its happening. "Finally, out of the ghetto" is the comment that I hear from them, but I'm not sure what all the attention means. The media are mostly interested in the family reunions. They want cute pictures of little girls dressed in Acadian costumes, of visitors from Louisiana serving up Cajun specialities: 5,000 EAT JAMBALAYA reads one headline.

There are so many aspects of the Acadian past, present, and future under the microscope at the university conference that an Acadian encyclopedia could be written just from the transcripts. There are something like three hundred presenters at the conference, but what they have to say is being largely ignored by the press. Much the same can be said for the cultural events: The plays from Louisiana receive no reviews whatsoever, but there are plenty of pictures of Acadian dancers. The nationalists grumble that this is all related to the desire to folklorize everything, but I can't help but feel that it has more to do with language.

I am the media, too. I am aware of its strengths and drawbacks when I record a radio piece for the CBC. On the one hand, I find it amazing that I can speak for two minutes in a studio in Moncton and my voice will be broadcast the breadth of an entire continent. Amazing and rather wonderful. On the other hand, as I talk to the producers in Toronto and I have to keep repeating my little piece over and over again to pare it down to the two minutes required, I feel that my words have become a radio version of the photo op.

Later, as I sit in the media centre at the university watching the various leading lights of Acadie giving their sound bites for the *New York Times*, the *Globe and Mail*, and so on, it strikes me that all of this is the puff of the moment. The interviews will pop up as feel-good pieces at the end of the evening news or on the front page of a newspaper section, and like cotton candy, the Retrouvailles will taste good for a few seconds and then vanish. Later you may vaguely remember the flavour was good but exactly what it was cannot be recalled. I keep thinking of the last words in the film *L'Acadie, l'acadie?!?* when a young girl, now no doubt my age, is asked "What is Acadie?" She responds from a well of fatigue after the demise of the university-student strike, "A detail, a detail."

I leave the media centre for the last time. I've decided to concentrate on my own Retrouvailles and leave the photo ops to others.

At lunch, I listen to a talk given by an Acadian lawyer named Warren Perrin, from Louisiana, who has launched a petition against the British Crown. It is a very clever move. He tells us that when the British-French war concluded with the Treaty of Paris in 1763, two Acadians went to London with a petition for King George III. The six-page petition asked that he declare formally that the exile of the Acadians was over. They were not granted an audience, and their petition went without reply. This is the first that I have ever heard of this petition, but its refusal had enormous consequences because it gave local British authorities in the colonies of Nova Scotia, New Brunswick, and Prince Edward Island continued authority to treat the Acadians as illegal aliens, to deny them land grants and to continue the persecution.

Warren Perrin has found this old petition and attached an amendment to it so that he cannot be accused of presenting an untimely request. He has personally given it to the British government via a consular office in the United States. The original petition requests that the exile be declared over and his amendment asks that a physical symbol be created to mark this occasion. In his speech, Perrin points out that under the terms of the 1755 deportation, which is still in effect because it was never rescinded, he is illegally in Canada.

To be both Acadian and Louisianan is a powerfully persuasive oratorical mixture. Perrin speaks of his children, who once thought their ancestors must have done something wrong to have been deported from Canada. Were they criminals? He quotes *Evangeline* – "The exile begins never to end" – as fluently as he does legal documents. He is motivated to see this old petition through to a successful conclusion by a need for justice and reconciliation, and to begin a process of reconciliation, it must first be admitted that a wrong has been done.

"Isn't it unjust that a people who took no part in a war, but suffered greatly from it, be excluded from the peace settlement?" His strong voice rattles the windows of the room like Louisiana rain. "The past can never be changed, but at least it can be dealt with honestly, not as it has been, as if it was some curious accident of history. It wasn't an accident. A colonial official deliberately took an illegal action in peacetime without the approval of his superiors or the British government, and that ain't right, pardner."

After his speech, he is surrounded by journalists asking questions. After all, how often does one see a 250-year-old petition being exercised? The Québecois journalists shake their heads; they find his quest at best quixotic. I suppose it is, but it makes perfect sense to me. The Acadian is nothing if not tenacious and stubborn – and we love to laugh. A man who can make you laugh is worth a lot of fence posts. But the memory that is most vivid is not of Warren Perrin but of an older man who came up to see this smart Louisianan lawyer after he spoke. The old man spoke in that familiar, broad Acadian accent which always sounds so easy on my ears. He said, "Your petition, it's all very nice, but if they won't finish it, why don't we? Someone should write to the English and tell them we forgive them, and be done with it."

In that sentence was all the humour, all the generosity, all the strength that has welded me forever to the Acadian cause.

FIFTEEN

The Marshes

He is well salted.

Anonymous

I'm glad that I chose to stay in Sackville. It is a quiet cove far away from the storm of socializing that is the Retrouvailles. As I stroll in the still of the evening down the tree-lined streets of this little town, it is difficult to believe that forty minutes away, there is a permanent red, white, and blue Acadian party going on. Here, all is tranquil. Sackville is a college town that is idyllic in summer. Its professors have all run away on foreign holidays, and its students have returned home, leaving behind peaceful streets and small, elegant, urban horizons.

At the bed and breakfast, the owner is looking a little anxious. Other French-speaking guests have arrived. "Would I oblige by making them feel welcome?" I turn to see a tall couple coming down the stairs. We settle on the porch to chat. They are Trahans from Québec. They have been touring Fort Beauséjour and the Minas marshes all day and have decided to stay here for the night. The Trahans once lived in Minas; the Doucets also. Almost all of Germain Doucet's grandchildren moved north to Minas from Port-Royal. They lived in what we would now call a co-operative, until the first dikes were built and they could afford their own houses. Are there Trahans in the Doucet genealogy? We compare notes. I think my line is pretty good because it goes back unbroken almost four centuries. Monsieur Trahan puts me to shame; he is able to trace his family back to the twelfth century in France. I shake my head. Germain Doucet came from a village in the Loire Valley, but the line before that is unknown.

"It's too bad that they lost Fort Beauséjour," says Trahan, looking towards where the fort still stands. "After that, we were sitting ducks."

I shake my head. "It's too bad they ever built it."

He smiles. "Maybe you're right."

The porch we are sitting on looks over a lane that leads directly to the marshes. Sackville, which lies along the edge of the Tantramar Marshes, has the same sense of tranquility as a village by the sea, only better. Here, not only is there the peaceful sense of sky and open horizons, but there is also a constant, gentle summer buzz of life: the sounds of birds settling down for the night, of small creatures rustling in the marsh grass, of cicadas sawing their evening song.

In the intimacy of the warm summer twilight, Trahan and I fall into a companionable conversation which has no beginning and no end, the kind of conversation that usually occurs only between old friends. A conversation that ebbs and flows along with the night sounds. If Acadie is just a detail, as the young woman said at the end of the film *L'Acadie, l'Acadie?!?*, then this evening is Acadie because it is just a comma in our lives, just a detail. But Acadie has been a conversation for four hundred years, and if a conversation is just a detail of human existence, then this is fine with me. There's more to life than the Arc de Triomphe. If I had to choose between gazing up at that noble edifice again and an evening like this one, the choice would not be hard. The Arc would lose.

The next morning, I decide to spend the day on the marshes. No one lives on the marshes. No one has ever lived on them. They stretch flat and rich and thick with grass around the Bay of Fundy and across to the Gulf of St. Lawrence. At Sackville, the marshes form the entire isthmus connecting Nova Scotia to New Brunswick. Three hundred years ago this land made the Acadians some of the richest farmers in the New World. The agricultural abundance of the drained marshes – the cattle, sheep, and crops of flax, barley, wheat, and hay – gave the Acadians farmers power, whether they wanted it or not. To have their armies dependent on the food grown by a potential enemy was unbearable to both the Bostonnais and the English.

Tomorrow is the opening of the Women's Summit, beginning with a speech by Antonine Maillet and followed by a gala gathering of political luminaries. But today I am going to play hooky. I pack a lunch, choose a book of poems, pick up a bicycle, and cycle down the lane to the marshes.

In January 1793, Louis XVI was beheaded by guillotine at Paris's Place de la Révolution, now Place de la Concorde. For some reason, I always think of this beheading when I visit the marshes. I have a vivid image of the executioner, Sanson, reaching into the basket and lifting up the king's still-pulsing head for the immense crowd to see. The neck was severed so quickly by the guillotine and the bleeding head snatched up by Monsieur Sanson so adroitly that for a few macabre seconds Louis Capet's eyes may have seen his own death and his ears have heard the immense cheer of the crowd.

The event was scrupulously reported because some twenty thousand people attended the king's death along with, of course, the media. The journalists reported that schoolboys threw their hats in the air with delight as the king's blood flowed; some people close to the action dipped pens, pieces of paper, and even their fingers in the blood. One happy participant was reported to have raised his bloody fingers to his lips, tasted the blood and said with satisfaction, "*Il est bougrement salé*" – he is well salted.

Perhaps he said this because the king's fondness for food was well known; he is always shown as being corpulent, even during the years of his captivity. But our happy participant may have said this because the king's beef came from the Breton salt marshes, where dike technology was first tried before being brought to the new world in 1632 by men such as Charles d'Aulnay, then governor of Acadie.

The Bay of Fundy marshlands proved more successful than those in Brittany. The low, flat coastal land combined with the very high tides around the Bay of Fundy meant that broad sweeps of the shore were exposed during low tide, an area so extensive that, once diked, it had the sweep of a prairie landscape. The Acadians simply called it the great fields, *les grands prés*.

I think about Louis XVI losing his head when I'm on the Acadian marshes because of the incongruity of the two situations, the peaceable kingdom of Acadie and the unchained violence of the Terror, being connected by the phrase, *Il est bougrement salé*. No doubt, the peaceful Acadian villages idealized in *Evangeline* were home to many contentions as well as virtues. The human condition is all cut from the same cloth, and no particular human society has an exclusive virtue or vice. Nonetheless, there is enough truth to Longfellow's poem to hold the myth he spun. Acadians were not war-mongering. They were one of the very few New World peoples never to fight with their aboriginal neighbours or to form a military alliance with them against others. There was the sense among the Acadians from the start that they had arrived not to conquer anyone, but simply to make a new life in the New World. They were a people changed by the New World environment into a society that did not want to contend for power, that would resolutely try to set its own terms of social engagement. And in 1713, after the Treaty of Utrecht, the Acadians collectively formally declared themselves neutral in the colonial wars between the French and the English.

But there was no escape from the war. From 1713 onwards, Acadie's neutrality became a political statement hotly disputed by the English, the Bostonnais, and the Canadiens. Neutrality wasn't an option. The terms of settlement in the New World were written in national struggles and class struggles for power that crushed neutrality. The later convulsions of the American and French revolutions were all about power and who should have it. The ugly death of the amiable Louis XVI came at the height of one of those periodic fits of barbarity which turn the human community into a butcher shop.

The blood of the French Revolution was dignified by the ideals of equality, liberty, and fraternity. And after a long, bloody military dictatorship and several bloody aftershocks, French society slowly creaked forward in the direction of those ideals. In this way, France has been enormously lucky, for most of the bloodbaths of mankind from

Oliver Cromwell's war against the Irish to the Nazi's gas ovens, from the genocide in Rwanda to the ethnic cleansing in the Balkans, have been distinguished by little except the size of the massacres. It is as if we human beings are only able to function for so long without killing each other; as if our internal wheels, no matter our religion, language, or culture, cannot keep spinning without bouts of collective assassination.

The Acadian marshes do not look like marshes, they look like pleasant fields, criss-crossed with reddish clay roads that are as soft underfoot as skin. It is only when you come to a stream and see the crevasse it has cut into the ground that you realize why there are no houses in the fields: under the surface, it is water. The barns here are built on stone stilts so that the water can flow under without rotting the foundations. The sea may be held behind dikes, but the land is only borrowed from it.

The place where the marshes end is marked by a gentle rise in the land and a line of farmhouses with barns behind, a line marking where the Acadian villages would have stood. Somewhere along it, Paul-Marie Doucet and his family once lived. It is a very peaceful country scene, of white clapboard houses and churches with simple steeples.

I park my bicycle against a grassy bank and find a comfortable place to sit. The ground is warm from the sun, and the clay soil soft. The day is silent except for the call of birds and the rustle of the wind through the grass. It is a good place to shed the bane of every traveller – too many

new things, too many new people "until the world seems
seasick with novelty," as Stendhal put it. I had started out
the day with the vague notion of crossing the marshes and
visiting Fort Beauséjour. It is open to the public and kept in
impeccable shape by Parks Canada; no doubt it is in better
condition than it was in 1755. But I can feel my ambition
to visit the place fading. I've driven by it many times, but
have never felt inclined to go inside. I probably never will.

For me, Fort Beauséjour represents an extension of the
guillotine. Its construction, defence, and capture were
rooted in the same incessant struggle for political domina-
tion that drives human beings as surely as a stream propels
a tiny twig along its surface. Fort Beauséjour is the place
the French raced to build in response to the English naval
base at Halifax. Beauséjour and the great fortresses at
Louisbourg, Québec City, and Ticonderoga formed a neck-
lace of defences protecting the land and sea routes to the
New France.

In the summer of 1755, Beauséjour was defended from
the English attack by about a hundred French soldiers. The
siege lasted a week or so before the two thousand militia
from Boston and the three hundred English redcoats over-
came it. When three hundred young Acadians were found
inside the fort, along with the French soldiers, Colonel
Charles Lawrence, the British governor in Halifax, finally
had the excuse he had been waiting for to claim that the
Acadian neutrality had been broken. He had a fleet of
transport ships already anchored in the bay and soldiers in

place. It was now or never to rid himself of these annoyingly independent people.

At the last minute, Acadian deputies raced to Halifax and agreed to take the full oath of allegiance and bear arms for the British. This little-reported last-minute conversion irritates both English and French historians. To the historians with French sympathies it says that the Acadians were unreliable as had always been suspected; to those with English sympathies it says exactly the same thing. What it says to me is that they were as they always proclaimed – themselves, not extensions of other national ambitions. And only when driven into the extremity of seeing their families divided, their homes burnt, their land taken, did their independence crack.

In Acadian French, we still use the word *lieu* – or place – for "raison d'être," or simply for "reason." Molière, the Marquise de Sévigné, and other seventeenth-century writers use *lieu* in this way also. Place gives meaning or context to life. A physical place is the basket in and from which meaning arises. The Marquise de Sévigné writes, "This story has no place" when she comments disparagingly on another writer's work. In 1755, the Acadians lost their *lieu*, their place, their raison d'être. As Maurice Basque said, it just "blew up." The explosion was not confined to one family's house or one village; an entire society "blew up" and was no more. The consequences of this are almost impossible to comprehend because for Acadians it was the end of meaning. The daily connections of family and friends, the cycle of the farming seasons, the sacred and secular celebrations, the sense of place, ownership – the entire, complex interdependence of a unique society vanished from the face of the earth. When Paul-Marie Doucet's parents, brothers, and sisters disappeared onto the deportation ships and he fled into the forest, his chance to grow up as Acadian ended. The story of the rest of his life was the story of his exile.

I lie in the grass, watching the clouds roll by. Tomorrow is the big opening of the academic conference. All the heavy hitters will be there: Boutros Boutros-Ghali, Jean Chrétien, the French ambassador. It should be interesting. Above, the clouds billow by, and I imagine each cloud to be a different people: the Chinese, the Americans, the Bengali, the Mi'kmaq, the Irish, the Gypsies, and so on. It is not such a difficult thing to imagine. We are all born human beings; the oceans of our common origin still flow in our veins – the nearest thing to human blood is salt water. It is only later we are shaped into peoples with mother tongues, religions, traditions, ways of remembering the past and imagining the future. It is only later we learn how to injure ourselves.

In the distance, I can see a farmer rolling his rich marsh hay into enormous plastic rolls ready for transport. The sweet salt hay from these marshes no longer fattens cows destined for human plates, but is shipped to the Gulf States to nourish the race horses of Saudi oil kings. More than two centuries have passed since Paul-Marie fled into the surrounding forest and the ships sailed away with his family, but here it feels no more than a whisper away, as if those days are as close as the warm summer clay beneath my feet. The Mi'kmaq call the marshes the belly button of the universe. The *nombril*. It feels that way to me, as if beginnings were as close as ends here. I take off my shoes and begin to walk back to town, bits and pieces of the past collecting around me like falling leaves.

SIXTEEN

———◆———

Antonine Maillet

Where people wish to attach, they should always be ignorant. To come with a well-informed mind is to come with an inability of administering to the vanity of others, which any sensible person would always wish to avoid. A woman especially, if she have the misfortune of knowing anything, should conceal it as well as she can.

Jane Austen, *Northanger Abbey*

For the Women's Summit the hall is packed with two, maybe three thousand women and a few dozen men. On my left, there are women from Louisiana, and on my right, women from Caraquet. I feel as if I'm wearing the wrong clothes, but settle down in my chair and try not to be obtrusive. We are all waiting for Antonine Maillet.

Antonine Maillet is not Jane Austen, but they share a surprising number of things. Size, for one. Both are tiny, delicate women. Antonine can't be more than five feet tall – when she speaks from a podium, she is obliged to stand on a stool so that she can see over the lectern. They are also both writers who capture the voice of an age. English country life will always have Austen as its great reporter. Acadie will always have Maillet as the one who put her stamp on *Acadie de la survivance*. The voice of La Sagouine has become the voice of Acadie emerging from the long trek begun in 1755.

Austen died in humble circumstances at age forty-two, living on the welfare of one of her brothers. She never did have a room of her own. Her manuscripts were written in the front room of the cottage that she shared with her mother and sister. Her bedroom was also shared. Her books were not published under her own name.

Fortunately, Maillet has lived long enough to enjoy the fruits of her work. She has been recognized not only with France's Prix Goncourt, but in many other ways. The signs on the Trans-Canada Highway announce you are now travelling through *le pays de la Sagouine*, the country of La Sagouine. A historic village has been constructed in the Bouctouche harbour, a replica of what La Sagouine's village would have looked like. Actors in period costumes animate it for tourists during the summer season. Maillet laughs and says the village is her revenge on her brothers, who when they were children wouldn't let her play in the cabin they had built in the woods. Now she has an entire village of her own. Antonine is the star of the reunion and is the opening speaker at both the Women's Summit and the academic conference.

Maillet arrives and doesn't wait on ceremony. She strides directly to the podium and launches into her speech without the slightest hesitation. She speaks with great brio, as if we have caught her in the middle of a conversation already begun. At first, I have trouble understanding; I hear the old accent so infrequently now. I hear the words but have trouble stringing them together. It is as if I have become a child again, and cannot understand the conversation of the adults. Then suddenly the words begin to click together.

Her speech sparkles, but what is she trying to say? I had guessed that she might concentrate on the role of women in Acadian history. Most of the mythic figures of Acadie are women. Two of them, Pélagie-la-Charette and La Sagouine, she has invented herself, but instead Maillet goes whirling back into the most remote past, past Longfellow's Evangeline, past the Acadian civil war between d'Aubray and Charles La Tour, past the brave Madame La Tour and the siege of Fort Saint John, past the first Acadian settlement, Port-Royal, in 1604, all the way to the first signs of life on the planet; to the cephalopods whose skeletons have recently been found in fossil stones on shores of the Bay of Fundy. Is she making fun of the Acadian habit of tracing genealogies back to the first Doucet, Maillet, or Leblanc to arrive in the New World? What does an antique life form have to do with a women's conference?

And then I realize that her speech is a long poem, a *chanson de geste* like the *Chanson de Roland*, but spoken in the rolling accents of old Acadie, a *chanson de geste* celebrating life. Her song connects the people of the earth to each other in a word-necklace of spoken sound. Once I realize this is what she is doing, her speech begins to make sense. She is saying that all the peoples of the earth, all the animals of the earth, even the tiniest shellfish have their own note to play in the song of the earth, and we must cherish each one, because without each of the earth's notes, the song of our home planet will be poorer. And in that song, the Acadian people have their own note. It is a great speech, and she has her audience smiling and laughing along with her.

The speech is not all idealistic. At the end, Maillet introduces a twist of Acadian realism, the sure knowledge that one day life will end for individuals and for nations also; that the universe is arranged in a way we cannot understand; that there are always ends as well as beginnings to everything.

"Why were we born humans instead of something else?" she asks. "If we must be born human, why are we born women and not men or vice versa? And why are some of us born with brothers or sisters or neither? It is not only death which is arbitrary. Life is also arbitrary. But within these hard outlines of the shell which defines our existence, we can take the time to tell stories and sing fine songs; we can love and be loved, and together help to form the symphony of our planet. If there is one central meaning to life on our planet, it is in making this music."

Waves of applause punctuate her speech and shake the air in the large hall. It is a poetic, wonderful speech, but my sense of the women around me is that, while they admire Antonine, they are not in awe of her. I am at the back of the hall where there are the usual seditious and ribald comments from the women around me. They make me smile. These women are from Louisiana, from New Brunswick, from Nova Scotia, they are the women who run school boards, create theatre companies, juggle budgets, negotiate marital and language discords, raise children; they are appreciative of, but not intimidated by, Prix Goncourt winners.

Jane Austen gave a modern voice to the notion of romance conquering all. Maillet has done something infinitely more complex. She has given a public face to women who have lived longer than the first blush of romance; women who have struggled with the consequences of romance, children, laundry, absent husbands, security, a sense of purpose and identity. La Sagouine is not a twenty-year-old Evangeline. She is seventy, and she has battled through romance, children, and the screams of middle age. But above all she is a woman. She is not an aesthetic extension of a world dominated by men, men as landowners, men as inheritors, men as admirals, men as scoundrels, men as honest angels. In Austen's world, women are always defined by their relationship to these great male powers. Will they be able to marry for love and money? Will they be obliged to quietly settle for less or nothing? These questions don't feature in Maillet's world. La Sagouine stands on her own feet, both physically in the play, and philosophically.

Maillet has given the women of Acadie their own house, and in so doing has expanded the entire society. The significance of her accomplishments comes from the fact that until the 1950s few Acadians were literate. My grandfather was as Acadian as it was possible to be, and he was illiterate. To understand him, you had to be with him. It was through talking that he passed on the values, language, point of view, and sense of history that went with being Acadian. And for most of human history this is all that people have needed.

Documenting on paper an external reality for your society was not necessary when people lived exclusively in small groups, and everyone knew the same stories of creation, kinship, art, and government. A Mi'kmaq in 1604 needed nothing more. For Chief Membertou, the first few Frenchmen who washed up on the Nova Scotia shore in their sailing ships were interesting curiosities. But once societies and languages begin to collide, it becomes essential to be able to understand your own society in more than an instinctive, reflexive way. Otherwise you risk your society being discounted and pushed aside by societies that possess writing and codified law, history, songs, all written down and labelled in English or French.

The manner of governing and civil discourse that people of an oral culture take for granted is not perceived as government by the intruding society because it is not recorded and packaged in law books. Literature that is spoken is not literature because it is not written down. Gines de Sepúlueda, the Spanish theologian, in his long justification for the murder of New World peoples includes the lack of writing in his rosary of reasons. "Not only have they no knowledge of writing, keeping no history except vague and obscure memory of things consigned to certain pictures, no written law but certain laws and barbarous customs. And they ignore the right of property." This lack of private property was, of course, incomprehensible for the Western social order, which was founded on who owned what.

Northern conquistadors used English instead of Spanish to record the faults of native North Americans but the concepts were exactly the same: child-like, inferior, requiring supervision, and so on.

Maillet's speech at the Women's Summit goes back to the time when people passed on culture, history, a way of looking at the world with nothing more than the human voice. The speech itself is so infectiously engaging, so embracing of others and life without ever relinquishing her own sense of being Acadian that I wish more people could hear it. I look for the omnipresent cameras, but there are none. It is too bad. At a time when the Canadian sense of nationality is riven with adolescent politicians playing destructive beat-the-chest games, we need to broadcast her luminous words.

She is so tiny that after the speech, when people crowd around her to have her sign a book or to take her picture, she completely disappears from view. I have spoken to her about my own radio project, and she has promised me an interview after the speech. As I approach the front of the hall to wait my turn, my stomach is churning with nerves. I've never produced a radio show before and I don't have a lot of confidence that I can handle the old Uher tape recorder that I'm carrying and at the same time engage in any kind of intelligent discourse. The Uher has a tendency to switch itself off automatically, forcing me to keep one eye on the ON button and the other on the sound levels. The hall is cavernous and with the audience breaking up it's going to sound like we're trying to talk in the middle of a thunderstorm. Can I ask a Prix Goncourt if she can move to some place quieter?

The crowd in front of her finally thins to two other reporters and myself. The other two are with Radio-Canada and Radio France. They look like they know what they're doing and they go first. The Radio-Canada reporter wants to know what the Retrouvailles means for the Québec referendum, which is coming up. Will it favour the federalists or the separatists? It is question that in one way or another all the reporters from Québec pose. They all seem to regard the Acadian community through the prism of their own preoccupations. I notice Maillet sighs slightly when she hears the question. It doesn't surprise her.

Some things endure for the centuries. From the Québec, or the Canadien, side of the fence, nothing much has changed since 1755 – the Acadians are still irritating, their behaviour still verging on traitorous. This time they are a problem because they won't take the loyalty oath to Québec. The Acadians are French speaking, yet they refuse to believe the gospel that the Canadian federal experience has been bad. Maillet negotiates around "the question" with the practised ease of an old campaigner, saying simply that she supports the official Acadian position that no bilateral agreement between an independent Québec and Acadie will be as powerful as a hundred French-speaking deputies in the Canadian Parliament. She refuses to elaborate further. The reporter looks annoyed, and hits his OFF button. His interview is over. My guess is that when his report is filed with Radio-Canada, it will sound like Maillet's speech was about the separatist referendum.

The image of the Acadian fox and the Canadien wolf comes to mind. The fox skips, giving offence to no one, but refusing to be trapped. Maillet is the fox.

The other reporters get their two-minute sound bites and go off to file their stories. The noise in the hall has dimmed a little, and Antonine Maillet is left staring blankly at me.

I introduce myself.

In the interview with Maillet I sense that she is tiptoe-ing around the same emotions as I am. I ask her when she thought the Acadian renaissance had begun and she explains that it was with the student revolt in the 1960s and the francophobe mayor Leonard Jones. "Sometimes I wish he would come back," she says and laughs. "It was Leonard Jones and Acadian artists, poets, novelists, play-wrights who made Acadie visible to the outside world and to ourselves. We are always coming out of the woods," she smiles when she says this. I want to say it is her work which gives so many young Acadian writers the confidence that they can be writers themselves. But I don't have the same courage as the Acadian women at the back of the hall. No doubt they could talk to Antonine with the casual brio of La Sagouine herself, but I find words hard to come by in her presence.

SEVENTEEN

Passez-moi le beurre, s'il vous plaît

1755 has become a point of reference for many Acadians. Although I personally did not live that deportation, my emotions have lived it – because I am the result of that event. My life on earth would have been totally different if my ancestors had not been deported. Most of the villages of modern Acadie are isolated and economically limited. My family was obliged to leave our village when I was five for economic reasons and that event is directly connected to Grand-Pré and 1755. My ancestors were deported from Grand-Pré.

Barbara LeBlanc

An ugly undertow is emerging at the academic conference. It centres on two questions. The first is, What is an Acadian? The second is, Where is Acadie? At first blush, both questions seem harmless enough. Every generation of Acadians must ask itself the first question because with every generation the answer changes. The second is just as complex and has no easy answers either. Is there such a thing as an Acadie beyond Maritime Canada? Can Acadie exist outside of New Brunswick or Nova Scotia? The debate is all about definitions, a subject I don't like because, although it's never quite said, it's all about who qualifies to call themselves an Acadian. There are no Acadian passports, no Acadian citizenship papers, so who qualifies? If your French has more than two mistakes per paragraph, does that discount you? If you live in Québec or Ontario, does that disqualify you? No one will come out and say it, but that's what the debates about place and language and public institutions are edging towards. It leaves me gritting my teeth for I can smell the acrid smoke of burning barns.

The front page of the Saint John *Telegraph-Journal* has a huge colour photograph of Jean Béliveau leaning down to shake the hand of an elderly person in a wheelchair. As a hockey player he had great class and he still does now. He still looks a star. The shade of his hair has changed, that is all. Béliveau and Richard are both old Acadian names, as old as Doucet. My cousin Roland takes great delight in reminding his Québecois friends of this connection: that the two great hockey players are just another couple of refugees from Acadie. It never mattered to me whether they were Acadian or Québecois, I never gave it much of a thought, but it mattered to me that they spoke French and wore the Canadiens' hockey jersey; that was important. Whenever I pulled on my own Canadiens hockey jersey, it felt as if I were pulling on a bit of my heroes; that they were sailing beside me as I skated.

I look at the picture of Béliveau and find myself overcome not with nostalgia but with a sense of mystery. How did something that used to be so important become so unimportant? Questions that could provoke a schoolyard fight are now scarcely remembered.

The morning sun is warm and pleasant and I feel sleepy. I'm sitting at a picnic table beside the university's gym, in a little corner of grass and sunlight, the newspaper heavy in my hands. I'm waiting to meet with Barbara LeBlanc. She's the director of Grand-Pré, the Parks Canada historic site that is kept as a memorial of the exile. But that's not the reason I want to meet her. I want to meet her because she is like me: she is Acadian, but she's never really lived in any Acadian region. I want to find out how it is she still thinks of herself as Acadian.

Jean Béliveau smiles up at me. He is no longer a painfully thin young man. His hair is grey and his hands incongruously large. The hands of hockey players are like those of workmen who have spent years manipulating pitchforks, shovels, axes, hammers. I notice in the pictures

I've seen of Maurice Richard that he holds his hands just like my grandfather did, hanging like spades from the end of his arms. The Rocket and Jean Béliveau were the two great athlete heroes of my childhood, Jean Béliveau for his grace and skill, Maurice Richard for his passionate game.

Was Rocket Richard the greatest hockey player of all? Greater than Gordie Howe? As a boy there was no doubt in my mind, it was Richard. Now I'm not so certain they are comparable. How do you compare Van Gogh to Rembrandt? There was only one Vincent Van Gogh and only one Rembrandt. Van Gogh's paintings were like jagged bolts of lightning across the polite world of salon paintings and yet the wrenching emotion he painted with mysteriously gives his paintings the gentle warmth of a man who greatly loved the world. You cannot look at his painting of a night sky by the café in Arles or his irises and fields of sunflowers and not know that this troubled man loved life. I think this is the reason people continue to admire his paintings. It is for the love of our little planet that shines through his fields of sunflowers.

Maurice Richard was the Vincent Van Gogh of hockey. He was a bolt of lightning on the ice, the fiercest, wildest of competitors, and at the same time a man of honest and simple warmth. If all the emotion of the game could be distilled into one human being, it would have the name Maurice Richard. Howe was more like Rembrandt. There was a calculating aspect to Gordie Howe's brilliant game which, combined with his enormous, athletic ability, made him close to invincible. Like Richard, he could skate through a whole team all by himself. But Richard's game was never calculated. It is not a calculated move to strike an official. It is not a calculated move to ask your coach to keep you out of the game because you've been up almost twenty-four hours moving your family from one house to another, and then when the coach insists that you play, to score five goals before collapsing. It is not a calculated move to play with a concussion and go into a convulsions at the end of the game.

Riots are not made around calculations. I was nine in 1955 when the great Montréal riot occurred because of Richard's suspension from the playoffs for striking an official. I remember watching on the television news the cars being turned over and the smash of glass. I was too young to understand why all this was happening; it seemed a little crazy for people to be hitting each other and breaking store windows and burning cars because of a hockey game. But children feel things with great intensity long before they understand them. The riot may have been a mystery to me but I knew that my sympathies were with Richard. I disliked the cold fish named Campbell who sat in the stands in his suit and tie. From such confused emotions, large, ugly mountains can be built.

Now I can explain my dislike in adult words. NHL commissioners have always been voices for the owners. There was nothing special about Campbell, and owning teams has little to do with concepts like fair play or passion for a sport, and everything to do with profitable manipulation.

Maurice Richard puts on his trousers one foot at a time like the rest of us. Perfection eludes us all because it implies stasis, and it is an immutable law of the universe that change is constant. But we humans do strive towards our odd notions of perfection, which are usually poorly understood but always cherished. To live in a just world. To be a better dad. To be a truer, wiser friend. To be a more supportive partner. To be a better employee, a better son, and so on. But perfection is never satisfactorily realized by anyone. No matter what our talents, it eludes us. But a very great athlete and a very great team can give vivid expression to that illusion. Maurice Richard and Jean Béliveau were the heart of one of those teams. For a few moments on the ice, they gave us the feeling that it was possible to win in the eternal struggle against chance and chaos. That it was possible to be perfect. Today, I feel nostalgic for them, yes, and also for my own boyish dreams of perfection. My greatest heroes are not generals or soldiers or movie stars, they're hockey players. In this way, I am utterly Canadian. Just seeing Maurice Richard walk slowly across the television screen, his hair now grey, but still with that unmistakable face and force of character, can bring tears to my eyes.

I don't know if this happens in English Canada, if hockey stars have this kind of meaning.

I look up from the paper to find a woman of middle height and age standing quietly in front of me. She smiles. She looks very self-possessed. We shake hands. "Barbara LeBlanc," she says with a smile.

She goes directly to the point. "Why do you want to speak to me?"

"Because I would like to know why you have come to the Retrouvailles."

She sits down on the other side of the picnic table from me. "Where do you want me to begin?"

"Where you want. Childhood. Adolescence. University."

"Too long. Let's start with after university. After university, I went to see what Europe was all about. I had a wonderful time, especially in Italy. I fell in love with the countryside and the language. I was only supposed to stay for the summer months and then come home and find a job, but I didn't want to come home. It would have been like finding the perfect cup of cappuccino and taking only one sip, so I stayed."

"How long?"

"About ten years, mostly working in the theatre. It was wonderful."

"Did you find it hard to learn Italian?"

"I lived and worked in the language. After a couple of years, people didn't know I wasn't a native speaker."

"What brought you home?"

"One day, we were sitting in a café, and the people I was with were talking about their roots, the towns they were from, their traditions and so on, which they were very proud of, and I realised with a kind of shock that I had my own roots, my own language, my own traditions. The more that I thought about it, the more I wanted to come home."

"You make it sound easy."

"It wasn't. Ten years away from your own country is a long time. Making the decision to come home was easy enough to do, but actually living the experience through was another thing entirely. It was much harder coming home than leaving. When I actually got home, I felt very confused. I hadn't spoken French since I was a child and had forgotten it long ago. All I could recall were a few phrases. My parents were happy to see me home, but they didn't know what I was about. As a child, once I had gone to the English public school I had refused to speak French in the house, and now I only wanted them to speak French to me. And I was always asking questions. Why did we leave Chéticamp? What was the Tintamarre? Why did Mother always make pâté at Christmas?

"My father would ask, 'why all these questions?' He didn't want to feel as if he was being examined all the time. It wasn't just me who was confused, so were my parents. They had spent a lot of time when I was a child trying to teach me about my Acadian heritage and language, and I had spent an equal amount of time resisting it to the point that I wouldn't even speak French to them. Now suddenly, I come home and the shoe is on the other foot. It was me who was pestering them to speak French and to teach me all the things that I had been so anxious to dump.

"It wasn't easy. I decided to go to Mexico. I told myself it was to learn Spanish, but in retrospect, I think it was to find some neutral ground. Some place that wasn't Canada, wasn't Europe, and wasn't the U.S. Some place where I could sort my confusions out. It worked. After a year there, I figured out what I needed to do. I came home again, but this time with a plan. I went back to university. I studied Acadian history, Acadian folklore, I relearned my French. Five years later I had a Ph.D. from Laval University and I was working at Grand-Pré. And that, in a very small nutshell, is it," said Barbara and she smiles at me again, as if daring me to take her seriously.

I can't help smiling back. "I still don't really know why you left the land of pasta to come home," I say.

"Maybe some things aren't entirely explainable. Why are you here? Why aren't you back in Ottawa doing whatever it is you do in Ottawa?"

I don't know what to say so I keep quiet.

"I think I know," Barbara replied for me. "It's called connections and community. I see it all the time. During the summer, we get thousands of tourists at Grand-Pré. Mostly, they want to see the place that Evangeline came from. It's a bit like tourists going to Prince Edward Island to see the house where Lucy Maud Montgomery lived. The church at Grand-Pré has the same feel as the Anne of Green Gables house. It's like an ornament from the past hanging around in the present. I'm not sure the Grand-Pré church has much to do with anything. Unlike Montgomery's house, it didn't even exist when Grand-Pré was Evangeline's home. Being director there is a bit like being an usher at a wedding that's been cancelled."

"Then why stay?"

"Because cancelled weddings still have guests, and the guests are interesting. I've noticed, for example, that the kids with Acadian names are not just interested in where Evangeline might or might not have lived, they are more interested in trying to make some sense out of Acadian history in a very personal way. These kids, many of whom speak French only haltingly, all feel this connection; they realize that their families ended up in Boston or Montréal or wherever not just by accident but because of this one central event. For them, Evangeline isn't just a legend. There is an Evangeline and a Gabriel somewhere in their own family history, someone who had been deported, separated from their family. When I realized this, I started writing about Acadian history myself, but from the perspective of a young person."

Barbara stops for a moment and we watch the big CBC trucks rolling up with the equipment for the gala opening of the academic conference this evening. This is the one Prime Minister Chrétien, Boutros Boutros-Ghali and other luminaries would be attending.

"Let me give you one other example of what I mean," Barbara continues. "When I was doing research for my Ph.D. here at the university, I came upon this man in the library. He was about forty years of age, from Liverpool, England, very well spoken and thoughtful. We got to talking, and he told me his story. His mother had an affair with an Acadian during the Second World War. She became pregnant. The soldier returned to Canada and the boy was raised in England. Later, she remarried and his stepfather became his father. One day, when he was seventeen, doing the kind of rebellious things that seventeen-year-olds do, his father said to his mother in exasperation, 'What do you expect from a bastard?'

"It was the kind of throwaway line that fathers can use in moments of anger, but the boy saw his mother's face when he said it. She went white, and he knew there was something more to it than just an angry moment. After some hesitation, he was told the truth. His mother had long ago lost all contact with his natural father. All she knew was his name and that he was an Acadian from Canada.

"The boy looked up Acadia in his school atlas and found nothing. There was no such place as Acadia. He wondered if his mother had been mistaken or if his father had lied about where he had come from.

"Over the years, he began to sort the story out and realized that at one time there had been a place called Acadia. He read Longfellow's poem and began to collect books on Acadian history. Slowly the idea formed of coming to Canada to see if he could find his father. When I met him at the university, he was researching his family history, looking for a man with his family name who would have been in England about the time his mother and father met."

"Did he ever find him?" I ask.

"I don't know, but if he does I hope the family's heart is big enough to find a place for him, because if it isn't he will find it hard." There is a silence between us, then Barbara speaks again.

"To me, connections are what these academic meetings and family reunions are all about. We're trying to expand the heart and soul of Acadie, back in time and also forward. Back to the places where we have come from and forward to the times to come. That's why we're here, to make connections with each other that we need to take us into the future, not just as individuals, but as a people. The speeches that we will hear tonight will be forgotten almost as soon as the cameras stop grinding, but the connections between people that are happening now, between you and me, between people from the States, from Ontario, from Québec, at family reunions in Shediac, Richibucto, Cocagne, and so on, they will endure. They will make a difference."

Meeting Barbara LeBlanc has a powerful effect on me. It is a greatly cheering thing to feel such a close connection to someone who I'd never met before and might never meet again, yet whose sense of exile mirrored my own. In that reflection I understood myself better. It struck me that diasporic Acadians have one thing in common that Acadians from Maritime Canada do not. For Acadians growing up in an Acadian village such as Cap-Pelé or Memramcook or Caraquet, there is no reason not to become Acadian because you are surrounded by the heart-beat of Acadie. This isn't so for Acadians outside of New Brunswick. For us, there has to be a defining moment, a subconscious click which changes things, otherwise it is inevitable we will just drift into the melting pot. For Barbara, that defining moment came in a café in the evening sunlight in Italy. For me, it came at the breakfast table at my grandfather's when I suddenly realized I could not even ask my aunt to pass me the butter in French. I stared at the butter for a long time and then I asked my aunt how to say "Pass the butter, please." And she replied, "*Passez-moi le beurre, s'il vous plaît.*" Those were the first words I remember saying in French.

Barbara makes me reflect more on the whole compli-cated concept of exile, the details of which are often hard to get beyond. There is a visceral emotional side, which is easy enough to understand and which, in one way or another, every exile feels. I have spoken French ever since I was twelve years old, but I've never been able to develop the grace that someone who has had an education in that language, or who has spoken the language from first mem-ories, acquires effortlessly. It's been a battle to educate my children in French, and the battle is not with anglophones, but with francophones who want to preserve their schools from the contaminating sounds of English in the schoolyard. I don't share this fear. I'd rather see fifty schools with English in the schoolyard and French in the classrooms than one *pure laine* school. Because I think the latter is the result of recession and fear, not opening and growing.

I once met an Acadian from southern Nova Scotia who had married an English girl with the last name of Ford. He decided to change his own last name, which was the Acadian family name Roy, to the English, Ford. He said with a smile, "A Ford is a Ford." Now people are amazed at how good his French is, not how bad it is. His exile was over.

Exiles aren't new, and the twentieth century has seen vast numbers of people displaced from their homelands. There are more reasons to experience exile than you can shake a stick at. There are religious exiles, economic exiles, literary exiles, self-imposed exiles, exiles at gunpoint – but there is one great line that divides an individual exile from that of an entire people.

The exile of a single person is an entirely different thing from the exile of a people. The exile of an individual is analogous to a skier plunging down a steep slope. The exile of a people is the snow itself crashing down the mountain in an avalanche. The skier traces a new path in the snow; the avalanche changes the face of the mountain. The exile of the Hebrews in Egypt and Babylon echoes within

Jewish people three thousand years later. The exile of the native people of North America by force, by religious and cultural oppression, is alive and with us today.

Whenever I want to gain perspective on the Acadian experience of exile, I think of the Mi'kmaq people. The Mi'kmaq and the Acadians share a great deal, not the least of which is our ancestors. At Eskasoni, a Mi'kmaq reserve not far from my father's village, you will find many Doucets, but their names are spelled Doucette. We were both oral societies that were only at home here in the New World. But unlike the Mi'kmaq, the Acadians had European origins. We spoke a European language and as a result, within a remarkably short time of returning, by the 1780s, Acadian fishermen had begun to petition the English authorities for recognition of land claims. They often had the support of English merchants who saw in the establishment of Acadian fishing communities the chance to make money. The Mi'kmaq people had no chance to develop the same reciprocity of interest with English merchants. The authorities continued to regard them not as neighbours or partners, but as problems to be dealt with. The crushing of their language and the dismissal of their political and religious systems make the Acadian exile look like the Cadillac version.

The experience of exile and refuge is so ugly that the urge is to run away from it, to forget that it has happened. But this is not the right thing to do. It is a rare family, regardless of its origins, that does not number refugees among it. The New World is the largest refugee camp in the world. Refugees from war and economic oppression throughout Europe, from war and famine in Asia, people exiled from Africa into slavery populate the New World. Exiles are created by the same process that creates national identities. Identity is a creative act of men and women, just as are exclusions from those identities. It is only possible to be un-American if it is possible to be American, un-Canadian if there is first a Canadian identity.

Exile is the reverse side of the nationalist coin and is as common today as it ever has been. Two hundred years ago, Acadians died on prison ships in English and French harbours, their crime being that they had no home. Today, Bosnians, Serbs, Croats, Kurds, Hutus, Dinka people languish in modern versions of those prison ships.

Exile was created in the triumphant sound of the guns of George Custer's 7th Cavalry, which even in defeat sounded the horn of victory, for it was the Sioux people who were exiled from their homes; Custer's compatriots who found homes.

The word *exile* has a round and deadly sound in my mouth. Who escapes?

EIGHTEEN

1755

The most popular band at the Retrouvailles is 1755. They were for years, along with Beausoleil-Brossard, the most popular rock 'n' roll band in Acadie, but time caught up with them and a whole new generation of bands came along to push them off the stage: An Acoustic Sin, Zéro° Celsius, Loup Noir. But 1755 has reunited just for the reunion, and their old songs are heard everywhere. The younger bands are going to have to take a back seat for the Retrouvailles. 1755's latest CD has a crimson cover and shows them standing on a stage in flames. 1755 is blazoned across the cover in a jagged streak of white that looks like something between a bolt of lightning and a flag. The flaming cover and the songs of 1755 suit the mood of the Retrouvailles perfectly. The CD flies off the store racks as fast as it is stocked. Barbara LeBlanc was right about that date; it resonates with all Acadians.

The date that sticks in the collective memory of the Québecois came four years later: 1759, *la conquête*. The

Conquest. The words feel bad in my mouth, like soup that
has soured. The curious thing is that 1755 was a much
greater disaster for the Acadians than 1759 ever was for the
Québecois, but when I say 1755 to myself, the words leave
no bitter taste. I do not associate it with defeat or conquest.
How can you be defeated if you never fought? The date, for
me, is like the white slash across the CD cover. It is the
marker I use to measure the tides of Western history, a date
to which all other dates are related.

The American Revolution came twenty-five years later,
in 1775; the French, thirty-four years later, in 1789. Molière
died in 1673, a century before the exile began. And so the
world turned from monarchy to democracy, from magic to
science, from craft to industry. In the space of the four centuries between 1604 and 1998, a great deal happened and
not very much at all. The great masted British men-of-war
have been replaced by nuclear submarines. The technology
has changed but the primitive purpose remains.

My father for one has always been a bit embarrassed by
the lack of the literate arts among his kin, about our distance from the great events and accomplishments of others.
Cajun, Cadien, the Bayou – the words have often been used
disparagingly as if Acadians were only half civilized. My
vision is different. It is as if I have a split screen in my head,
each showing a different version of reality. In one the
importance of reading and writing just slips away. There
were desultory efforts to set up a school in Port-Royal by the

Capuchins. But the school faded away after only a few years. So what?

The Acadians had left behind the Old World, the old institutions, the old power structures, and were beginning a new society, a new way of living that was democratic, creative, and engaged. And they could not have found a better place to do it. When Molière was writing *Le Malade imaginaire* and fighting poverty, illness, and for royal patronage, the Acadians were settling into a place that was as close to Eden as can be found on our planet. Their villages were growing beside a magnificent salt bay so alive with cod, mackerel, lobster, scallops, it was enough to build a wicker weir and let the receding tide fill it with fish. The seasonal round was gentle, the land ornamented with majestic forests, the coastline gently sloping to the sea in wide stretches of saltwater marshes.

In 1654, when Germain Doucet returned to France, his children and grandchildren were busy building new dikes to wrest the marshes from the sea. They were busy devising new community structures, adapting technology, learning from the Mi'kmaq, creating a new kind of society. They were flourishing. A hundred years later, in 1759, the Acadians were in refugee camps; they were domestics in rich people's homes; they were hiding in isolated fishing coves; they were on the run.

In four hundred years, there have been at least five Acadies. The first one was dismantled in 1755. What it might have become, we can only speculate. Perhaps a kind of French-speaking New England, with conservative politics, pleasant colleges, and a dark streak of Puritanism. Or would it have developed into a different kind of society entirely? One in which the Mi'kmaq people would play a central role and not have been marginalized? Who knows? What we do know is that Canada would be a different kind of country if 1755 had never happened. Canada would be a more bilingual, bicultural nation because there would have been at least one other French-speaking community with an imposing national presence. The isolation from the national scene that many Québecois feel would have been attenuated by the voice of a strong but different French-speaking community in the national discourse.

The second Acadie was the Acadie of the survival. *L'Acadie de la survivance*, the period between 1755 and the first national Acadian gathering of 1881. It was during this time that the survivors of the Deportation re-established themselves mostly along remote stretches of the Gulf of St. Lawrence from Caraquet to Chéticamp. These were the years when Acadie was reinvented, quietly, surreptitiously, away from the prying eyes of the English. It came out of hiding with the first national convention at Memramcook. Suddenly the Acadians were back, choosing a national flag and putting together a skeletal national organization that would enable them to talk to each other and help each other beyond the boundaries of each fishing village.

In 1881, Acadie began to change into a third Acadie, la Nouvelle Acadie, the New Acadie. For the first time, a small college was established at Memramcook. A small community of secular scholars began to form around the college but in the end this renaissance was still born. An Acadian senator, Pascal Poirier, was appointed to the federal cabinet. He became a great advocate for Acadie on the national scene and the author of a series of books, the most important being *Le Glossaire Acadien*. For the first time, the Acadian language had a dictionary that distinguished it from the French of both France and Québec. Monsieur Poirier did not like the Académie Française, and his glossary is full of disparaging remarks about how the Academy members are jumped up *arrivistes* who took a Paris dialect and relentlessly imposed it on the popular language, forcing out words, phrases, verbs, imposing spellings, genders, and so on. Poirier never loses an opportunity to point out that Acadian French is pure seventeenth-century Loire Valley French and its words and manner of expression can be found in the plays of Molière. If a glossary can be described as a wonderful, gossipy read, Poirier's glossary is.

Poirier lost the glossary twice, first in 1887 in a house fire at his brother's in Shediac. All of his papers and books were destroyed, including his history of Acadie and his research notes from Boston, London, Paris, Ottawa, and Montréal. He was never able to reconstitute this history, but he put himself to work again on the glossary. He lost it a second time in the great fire that destroyed the Houses of Parliament in 1916. He began working on it a third time. Pieces of it were published in a newspaper but it was never published in book form during his lifetime.

The third Acadie stumbled and died in the Depression of the 1930s. It died because it was fragile from the start, narrowly based in a few New Brunswick towns, mostly at Memramcook. When the hurricane of the Depression hit North America, the Acadian villages were still isolated, with few institutions, little material wealth, and little communication with the outside world. The Depression threw Acadian villages back onto a barter-subsistence economy. Banks closed. Fish plants closed. Credit and markets evaporated. Schools and hospitals turned to religious orders to operate. It was as if a giant hand had come down across Acadie, strangling businesses, public projects, and communications with the outside world. Another difficult period of survival began. Priests in their parish halls and in colleges such as St. Francis Xavier promoted the co-operative movement. The credit union that was started in Grand Étang to replace the departed bank was begun with pennies deposited in the village presbytery. This was typical.

The start may have been shaky, but the notion of co-operative economic institutions took root with surprising speed. It did not take much convincing for people to begin to create co-operative banks (credit unions), fish plants, dairies, and marketing agencies. By 1950, a new institutional structure across Acadie had emerged that could finance projects and market goods, and there was a new generation in place ready to take Acadie in a new direction. The generation of young men and women who had left for the Second World War came home and educated themselves using the Veterans' Bill, my father among them. But the effects of 1755 still lingered. The communities were not diverse enough to absorb a generation that was suddenly highly educated. There were no slots for lawyers, economists, accountants, and so the majority of this generation took their educations and experiences to the cities: Boston, Montréal, Toronto, Vancouver. They didn't come home. Their villages were too small.

The 1940s and '50s were a curious time in Acadie. It was as if its villages were becalmed. Life went on. Roads were paved. Families were formed. Fishing boats got bigger. Television arrived. Banks quietly moved back in. New business started. And small farms like my grandfather's disappeared. Life went on. Nothing was wrong but there was an unnatural quietness. The war and the departure of so many the young had let the air out of an entire society. Once more, Acadie was struggling. This time not against poverty and isolation, but for a sense of itself.

At the end of the 1960s my generation suddenly found its feet, and the fifth Acadie began to take shape. A francophobe mayor named Leonard Jones inspired a revolt at the Université de Moncton, and Acadie discovered for the first time that it had an urban centre, and its name was Moncton. From 1968 on, it would be the capital of Acadie.

The artists, the publishers, the filmmakers who gathered at the university, and the businessmen who gathered around the co-operative headquarters gave Acadie a modern window both on itself and on the world. In the 1990s, when the Retrouvailles were being organized by some exiles in Edmonton, there was no question where the centre should be. Moncton.

Can a society ever recover from something as devastating as a forced exile? The simple answer is, with time, anything is possible. But even today nothing happens in Acadie that is not marked by 1755. It is a wind that still blows.

———•———

The world is full of refugees, and Canada has opened its doors more than most. Maillet's Pélagie, struggling back to Acadie with her little cart, has many companions. The Irish escaping famine, Highland Scots pushed off their land, street kids escaping London and Glasgow, Armenians, Somalians, Mennonites, Hutterites, Jews, Lebanese, Ukrainians, Doukhobors, Chinese, Poles, German Catholics, Vietnamese, British Loyalists, and draft dodgers from the States; if you go back far enough, most Canadian families have among their ancestors refugees from war, religious dispute, or poverty. The Acadians are not alone in their troubled past. I would like to think this has helped form our national character, which is famous for its sense of nuance; our willingness to listen to the other guy; to play the role of peacekeeper; to support a nationalism that promotes harmony and social justice rather than conquest.

A nation is not a consumer item; it is an invention held in the air by the people who live there, an expression of the collective will of each and every one of us. Canada is Canada because its citizens chose it to be so. It is different from other nations because of choices we have made, choices we are making, and choices that we will make. National programs such as medicare do not exist by some external executive fiat, they exist because Canadians chose them and Canadians pay for them. Carrying firearms in Canada is a privilege, not a constitutional right. It is this way because we chose it. We used to spend a great deal of money on our public schools because we believed them to be great integrative, progressive institutions in which all Canadian children could get a fair start. My fear is that too many people are forgetting these simple things, and that one day we will wake up and discover we have a country that is not as complex, or as interesting, or as humane as it has been. We will wake up to something we do not like. And people will wonder what happened and demand to know who did it. The answer will be simple – we did it.

For Acadians, the spirit of 1755 is not the spirit of conquest or defeat. It is the spirit of endurance in the face of great adversity, of strength, not power, of courage, not despair, of caring for one another, of prosperity, not parasitism. It is the kind of spirit with which Tommy Douglas brought in medicare. This is the best of Canada, a country that has tried to care for all of its citizens, not just in word but in deed, regardless of their colour, language, religion, or material circumstance. If I have a wish, it is that 1755 be connected to Canada in this way; that Canadians remember old Acadie and its values, which were about caring, not winning.

NINETEEN

———•———

Definitions

The word poreux in French means *full of holes. I think
"porous" is the same thing in English. I wanted to make a
pun, a kind of play on words. Starting with the idea l'Acadie
is full of holes, we have to decide whether l'Acadie is going
to be l'Acadie diasporique, with all the constructive part of
it – or are we going to be l'Acadie diasporeuse, with all the
negative part of it, all the disillusions, and maybe disappearance at the end.*

*It's very mixed up. Some people say "L'Acadie is the
Acadian peninsula in the north" and they mean it! They say
l'Acadie is nothing more than a small corner of northeastern
New Brunswick. I've heard people from Caraquet say,
"L'Acadie, you know, Calixte, is Caraquet"; and some people
say l'Acadie is New Brunswick; and some people say l'Acadie
is les provinces maritimes; and people from Louisiana,
when they come here and they hear that, well: "Listen, we
have l'Acadie down here too."*

It's not clear what Acadie is; it's a floating notion. That's why I used the words fouillis epouvantable *(appalling jumble), which is very shocking. But I think they got the message because they talked about it in the papers for days after.*

Calixte Duguay, Poet, Musician, Composer

A t the launch of the academic conference, the stage is loaded like an Italian wedding cake with row upon row of dignitaries. Television lights bathe them in unnatural brightness, making them glow. There are several thousand people in the audience. The evening has barely begun and the sports centre is already hot. I'm sitting not too far from the stage in a group of reporters. Around me, people are recording for radio, scribbling for the newspapers, and rolling videotape for the various networks. The lead hitter on the stage is Antonine Maillet. Her speech is partly a reprise of the speech that she made earlier at the Woman's Summit and partly new material. It doesn't have the same power. It is as if the speakers queued behind her, waiting their turn to speak, weigh her down. Her speech, instead of being energizing, sounds forced, as if she is shovelling the words at us. There needs to be a synergy between the audience and the speaker as there was for her at the Women's Summit, but this time it isn't there. Behind her, waiting to rumble down the runway to the podium, are Boutros Boutros-Ghali, the Secretary-General of the UN, then the French ambassador, then a Québec minister pitch-hitting for Jacques Parizeau, then the premier of New Brunswick, Frank McKenna, then Prime Minister Jean Chrétien. Maillet is a storyteller, and storytelling needs time and space, neither of which she has here.

The evening is very political. Boutros Boutros-Ghali makes the United Nations point, in impeccable *lycée* French, that it is possible to be a people without having an army and political borders. He says that the Acadians have made this clear. He says it is no accident that the UN considers this first World Congress of Acadians to be a cultural event of worldwide significance.

Not surprisingly, Jean Chrétien uses the occasion to make the point to the Québec journalists that he is speaking French to a French audience and he isn't in Québec. The Québec journalists are expecting this and they grimace. I have the impression that, in spite of their superficial grumpiness, this is what they are most comfortable with, and they highlight with neon markers the sections of the prime minister's speech that defend federalism. It's like watching a tennis game between Chrétien and the Québecois journalists that was choreographed decades earlier. Their stories are written as soon as the prime minister opens his mouth. Rumpled Jean Dion, who writes about the rest of Canada for *Le Devoir*, looks like a choirboy contemplating a particularly pleasant sin. I think he could write his story in his sleep.

The minister from Québec announces that Québec will be opening an office in Moncton that will cost more than a million dollars and involve some permanent jobs, always a popular idea in New Brunswick. His speech is admirably short and to the point, which is that Québec is the only French-speaking political jurisdiction in North America and it is investing in this special way in Moncton, even though the Québecois are not fond of Acadian federalist sympathies. Point well taken.

Plus ça change, plus c'est la même chose. Two hundred and fifty years after the exile, the politics of larger nations still swirl around Acadie. The audience is good humoured. They are enjoying the attention of these great ships of state that float personified before them, but I don't think there are any illusions in the crowd. Tomorrow will come, the cameras will go, and it will be back to the daily *train-train*, meantime the show is fun.

During the speeches I look at my Québec colleagues. Is it my imagination or are they gazing beneficently down from their ramparts? One of the differences between Acadians and Québecois is that we have no stone ramparts, no cannons, no Plains of Abraham, where a French general was defeated by an English general. The Conquest of 1759 is the watershed that divides Québec into a before-and-after society. I've never been able to see it that way. For me, the defining symbol of Québec is unchanged since the days of New France. It is that of the Citadel besieged: the Bourbon King's blue-and-white fleur-de-lys flying over the Citadel of Québec. This image predates the conquest and it is enshrined in Québec history books in the stories of famous governors such as Champlain and Frontenac. It continues today with the blue-and-white fleur-de-lys still flying above the stone walls of the Citadel, and in a more prosaic way on every Québec licence plate with the words *Je me souviens*. I remember. I remember that we are a fortress people. I remember that we have defended ourselves. I remember we have fought for our place in the New World and know that we always must.

Québec's stance remains that of a citadel besieged. This was the creed of the Canadiens before 1759 and would have endured if Montcalm had won and Wolfe had lost.

Historically, the differences between Québec and Acadie can be seen most vividly after the conquest of 1759. The terms of capitulation guaranteed the Canadiens property rights, freedom of worship, the position of the clergy, a Catholic education, and the Montréal merchant community (the North West Company) was assured equal access to the rich fur trade of the western part of the continent. The principal inconvenience for New France was that its military regiments had to be disbanded.

By the time Montcalm and Wolfe were firing cannonballs at each other, the Acadian deportation had been going on for four years. All Acadian property, except what could be carried on people's backs, had been seized and would be for another four years until the war officially ended in 1763. The fabric of Acadian society was being torn from the landscape. In the worst position of all were the Mi'kmaq, who had a bounty placed on their heads and were hunted, not just for their property, but for their lives. In 1759, when the Canadiens and British signed the agreement ending hostilities in Montréal, no mention of the Acadian exile or the Mi'kmaq scalp hunt was made. Neither were relevant to the lawyers and military officers who devised the agreement.

The differing treatment of the Canadiens and the Acadians is usually explained by the fact that the Deportation came near the beginning of the 1755–63 war, and the Battle of the Plains of Abraham marked the end. By then, all the great French fortresses, Louisbourg, Beauséjour, Ticonderoga, and finally the Citadel itself, had fallen. I have never thought the explanation was that simple.

England and New England, France and New France were closer to each other, not just in size, but in organization and philosophy than Acadie ever was to France or England. It wasn't difficult for an English colonel and French colonel, an English bishop and a French bishop, an English fur merchant and a French fur merchant, a British lawyer and a French lawyer to find both points of conflict and of accommodation. Their educations, class, and professions had a great deal in common. Once religion and language were stripped away, a natural reciprocity of interest bounced to the surface. In modern parlance, both the English-English and French-French elite were interested in cutting a deal that would be mutually beneficial. Neither was interested in an ugly, punitive scene in which both sides would lose.

The English elite wanted unfettered access to the continent's vast resources with the compliance and assistance of the local Canadian elite. The Canadian elite wanted their property and religious systems maintained. Each elite fed off the other. Each did well.

The Acadians did not belong to this old network. They had no General Montcalm, no Old World attachments. From the capture of Port-Royal in 1654, Acadie had been cut off from both England and France. The English tried to govern from Boston, the French from Versailles. Neither worked. The English were busy in New England and what little resources the French had went to Québec. After 1713, the Acadians grew quite used to living under an English king – but not to the point where they wanted to start carrying guns. Nor did they have any local elite to encourage them to get on the "right" side; no clerical class, no bishops, no Monsignors, no North West Company, no merchant princes, no colonels to negotiate mutually beneficial agreements, and as a result the English governors could only imagine two political scenarios: either the Acadians owned the land and continued to control the wealth of Acadie, or they were displaced and English settlers ran the show. In this way, the Acadians were treated like the Mi'kmaq. The principal difference between the

English view of the Mi'kmaq and the Acadians was that exile was not deemed possible for the Mi'kmaq. Physical eradication was the only solution.

But in the twentieth century, in one of those ironic twists that history is full of, the political sides have switched. Now it is the Acadians who are willing and able to find a compromise with the English-speaking majority, and the Canadiens (the Québecois) who are not. For the Québec separatists, federalism has become a zero-sum situation, us or them, and the Acadians have become *les petits vendus*, the sellouts. Everywhere I go, I overhear the Québec journalists talking about the upcoming referendum vote on Québec sovereignty. Acadie's only importance in their eyes is how we may affect the outcome of this vote. They do not seem capable of imagining Acadie on its own terms, within in its own history, within its own Tintamarre.

———◆———

The great controversy of the conference is not the politics of the gala, it is around the speech of Professor Joseph Yvon Terriault. The university professors of Acadie have become the new priests; they carry the nationalist and cultural flag that the church used to. Terriault is head of the sociology department at the University of Ottawa, and he has come to the conference prepared to take on artists such as Antonine Maillet and Calixte Duguay. Maillet's famous line "wherever there is an Acadian, there is Acadie" has always been central to the Acadian sense of identity. It is the definition of Acadie that applies to Evangeline and Gabriel and their figurative children, but Professor Terriault isn't buying it. He considers this concept of Acadie verging on destructive. Terriault thinks it's charming to meet someone from Louisiana with a name the same as his own or to hear about the success of artists such as Maillet and Duguay in Montréal, but a society is not constructed out of the lives of individuals. Like the good academic he is, Terriault begins his speech by defining what he considers a civil society to be. For this he uses Diderot's definition: a political body of men (and I presume now women) of the same situation, the same city or another place forming an ensemble of political attitudes which attach one to another.

The foundation of a civil society has nothing to do with religion or what your family name happens to be. And this civil society, Terriault contends, can only be found in Maritime Canada. He says, "I live in Ottawa, and I can assure you there is no Acadie in Ottawa." This sentence flies in the face of Maillet's definition of Acadie and rings around the conference.

Terriault's speech is academic and dry. In the cavernous hall, it is hard to follow, but unlike the familiar bromides of the eminent politicians, the content is dynamite. Acadians have not had a territory since the Treaty of Utrecht in 1713 and have been on the move since the 1755 deportation, the majority living outside of Maritime Canada. Rebuilding that civil society Terriault speaks about has taken the resources of Acadians around the world. Diderot's civil society has steadily grown in Acadie. There is now a French-language university and French-speaking professionals in the towns and villages of Maritime Canada. The rebirth of Acadie has continued, but Terriault is drawing a line in the sand and saying that there is only one Acadie possible, that the old definitions no longer apply.

After the speeches I get a chance to interview the rector of the Université de Moncton, Jean Bertrand Robichaud. Like Terriault, he speaks in an academic but very direct way. He doesn't mince his words: "What the World Congress is saying is that l'Acadie is not l'Acadie of the Maritimes, because there are, at most, three hundred thousand Acadians here. If it's true that there are three million Acadians worldwide, then there's ten percent of Acadians here in the Maritimes. I think the impact of this Congress on l'Acadie is going to be very, very important. I think it's going to be hard, it's going to be tough, it's going to be painful, but I think it's going to be positive. Because it forces a redefinition, basically of the ideology, of the discourse, of the way people think about themselves and the way people relate to each other."

Yvon Terriault is the leading edge on one side of that discourse. He does not mince his words either. "When I said, 'I live in Ottawa and I can assure you there is no Acadie in Ottawa,' I was saying that maybe there are some people like me who are Acadian and who live in Ottawa, but there are no social relations in Ottawa that will recreate and transmit Acadie. A society is a society when we have the possibility of transmitting a way of living. I will not transmit this way of living to my children, because we are not living in a strong enough social tradition to give them this heritage, this transmission of a way of life. They will receive a French-Canadian culture but not an Acadian culture. They are not living in an Acadian environment, an Acadian network."

The last person I interview after the gala is the playwright and composer Calixte Duguay. He has been a creative force in Acadie for a generation, touring the villages of Acadie first as a singer and later with his plays. I can remember him in Grand Étang performing in the grounds beside the church. He is one of the artists who carved out a path for wider success that many young Acadian artists have followed. First you become known in your own village, then you tour the villages of Acadie. If the tours are successful, there is the chance for a recording contract and the hope of springing into the international scene. In Moncton, Duguay is directing a lavish revival of one of his early plays. Duguay's childhood home is Caraquet, but he has lived and worked in Montréal for many years.

This is what he has to say in the debate over what he believes Acadie to be: "I wrote a song years ago called 'Les Aboiteaux.' *Les aboiteaux* were the symbol of old Acadie. They were the channels that were cut through the dikes to

allow fresh water to drain from the fields into the bay so
that the land would not become waterlogged behind the
dikes. If the *aboiteaux* or the gates (*clapets*) that controlled
the flow of water through the dikes broke, everyone had to
go and repair them. Then they made a big party after.
When I prepared my speech, the *aboiteaux* took on another
face; they became a metaphor for the movements of artists,
Acadian artists especially, who leave New Brunswick for
Montréal or somewhere else in order to further their art,
and then return.

"I felt for a long time that the flow of people from
Acadie was like the flow of sea water through the *aboiteaux*,
that it was necessary, and probably Antonine Maillet and
Edith Butler felt that way too. Some people would say that
we were traitors – traitor is a bigger word in English – that
we have in some way become traitors because we left
Acadie.

"I don't see it that way. Poets and humanists have for
thousands of years dreamed of a *pays sans frontières*, a
country without borders, because we know that frontiers are
a source of division, of war. L'Acadie, in a certain way, is *un
pays sans frontières*. There's no frontier. If you're from
Louisiana, you're an Acadian. If you're from Montréal,
you're Acadian. If you're from New Brunswick, you're an
Acadian. It's special in this way.

"Acadians have been able, through all these years, to
maintain a new form of culture, original and pertinent to
the people here and to the people at large, which is called

l'Acadie; the kind of culture that has a bit of sadness in it. When we look at the writing, song, poetry, or painting, there's always a kind of sadness and nostalgia, which is probably influenced by the history of the people.

"This Retrouvailles is a great thing because for the first time we are seeing the two Acadies side by side. The Acadie of New Brunswick and the Acadie of the diaspora. I think we all hope that it will be a meeting that is creative and useful and not argumentative and destructive. But it will be a while before we see what soup there is to be made from it."

My interviews are over. The huge cavernous hall is dark. The VIPs have long since been whipped away to a reception. My T-shirt is damp with sweat, not just from the heat of the evening, but also from the emotion. The sentiments expressed in the speeches have each in their own way been persuasive, but there has been something unhealthy on the prowl. The Retrouvailles have brought more than world leaders to Moncton. They have also brought the powerful beast of nationalism, power, and money here. It is circulating the crowd, looking to dine on Acadian crumbs. And it hasn't been just those "from away" who have brought the beast. It is the first time that I have come across this in Acadie and it makes me uneasy.

Where is Acadie? Who is Acadian? Am I Acadian?

TWENTY

Villages Along the Water

I grew up in Grand Étang, Inverness County, Nova Scotia, on the island of Cape Breton, in a big white house. My mother's from Chéticamp, my dad's from Grand Étang, so the tensions between the two villages were kind of resolved in my household – or exacerbated, one or the other.

It's a small fishing village along the water: our house was about a football field away from the ocean. You can see the mountains in the other direction. In the spring and summer you could hear the ocean from my bedroom when the window was open. We had cows and pigs and chickens.

Roland Doucet

I decide to finish my retrouvailles by driving along the coast on the old highway, dropping in on family reunions as I go. The Doucet family reunion is at Richibucto, a fishing village on the Gulf shore about an hour from Moncton, but first I stop at Memramcook, the oldest continuously occupied village in Acadie. This is where the first Acadian college was located and where Governor General Roméo LeBlanc was born. It was also the place Pascal Poirier was educated.

The village of Memramcook lies on a height of land overlooking one of the tidal estuaries of the Bay of Fundy. From the college, you can see the old Acadian dikes snaking along the edge of the Petitcodiac River like ancient memories, but they no longer shelter fields behind them. The land around Memramcook is now simply marsh, miles and miles of flowing grass. The gates that once controlled the flow of tidal water have long since disappeared. Some of the *aboiteaux*, which cut through these dikes, are timbered tunnels six feet high and four feet wide, capable of funnelling an impressive amount of water in and out, but the oldest ones are quite small, no bigger than a large tree-trunk. Memramcook is one of the very few villages that Acadians were allowed to resettle after the Deportation and as a consequence, it has always considered itself to be the capital of Acadie, the natural inheritor of Port-Royal. Many distinguished graduates of Memramcook's classrooms have decorated the national scene.

The Université de Moncton has replaced the old college, and it is now used as multi-purpose community and conference centre. I discover a concert going on on the third floor, a children's music class. The boys are all dressed up in white shirts and grey flannel trousers, the girls in grey skirts. As I enter, a boy and a girl are playing "Jesu Joy of Man's Desiring." The familiar notes float up to the ceiling. I have never heard the tune sound more entrancing; not the execution itself, but the expression of the meaning, which is the ancient yearning of humankind for perfection. I have the curious feeling that Bach is sitting here at the back of the room with me and that he, like me, is smiling.

Downstairs, I look for some of my books in the bookstore, but there are only books in French. I introduce myself to the manager who has never heard of me, even though at least one of my books is on the New Brunswick English-school curriculum. I explain that even though I write in English I consider myself an Acadian writer. She looks amused at this notion. She says very politely that there are many places you can buy books in the English language but only a few where you can buy French. Delicately put, but the point is crystal clear; she has no intention of stocking *The Priest's Boy* or *My Grandfather's Cape Breton* in her store. It is a vivid reminder of the line language draws between people.

Richibucto reminds me of Chéticamp. It is a fishing village whose face is turned towards the sea. All the houses face the harbour, where the boats are modern-day equivalents of the dikes of Acadie. They are the means of earning wealth. Richibucto has the same scrubbed feeling of all Acadian villages. If the devil was dust he would have a hard time here. The houses are all freshly painted; the gardens neat. For Sunday afternoon promenades down by the harbour there is a wooden boardwalk which winds its way along the water's edge, and there are little cabins where you can buy ice cream. Richibucto, like Chéticamp, has discovered tourists. They are important. They bring the outside world to the villages and they bring demand for new services, for campgrounds, golf courses, summer theatre and so on – services that give new dimensions to a fishing village.

In the 1950s, Chéticamp and Grand Étang were as isolated from the mainstream as any Indian reservation. The connections to the outside world were just beginning. The Cabot Trail had recently been paved and is now an all-weather road, but people in Grand Étang were used to living as if the world ended at Kelly's Mountain. In winter, the old gravel road was often closed completely and all shipping stopped, the coastline frozen with pack ice. It was as if the clock had been rolled back two hundred years. Grandfather was so Acadian, he would have fit into the village of Grand-Pré or Beaubassin without a blink. He would have known or quickly learned what needed to be done, and his accent would have been right.

There are several family reunions going on in Richibucto. As the Doucets are one of the smaller Acadian families, our reunion is being held in conjunction with the Vautours'. "Small" among Acadian families is a relative term. The reunion is being held in Richibucto's hockey arena. There are over fifteen hundred people here. At one end of the hall, there is a corner where people can complete genealogical searches using computers. The twentieth century comes to Jean à Joe à Petit Tom.

In the middle of the hall, a band plays, and at the far end, vendors are selling souvenirs. I buy T-shirts for me and my children. I want them to be reminded that the Doucets are connected to people and places, a history and ways of thinking about our place in the world, but I am no longer sure just what that place is. While I am sure Grandfather could have adapted quickly to life in Beaubassin in 1740, I'm not so sure he could have moved forward thirty years from his own time to 1996. Nor do I agree that the French language is the defining characteristic for Acadians. There are millions of people who speak French around the world, North Africans, Asians, Haitians, Parisians; they are not Acadians. A sense of people has to come from more than a language. A language is both a passport and a filter through which people feel and express the world. The reason we use the terms anglophone and francophone today is because they indicate a manner of expression but not a cultural identity. For there are other qualities – landscape, climate, music, stories, friendship circles, traditions, philosophies – that define a people.

Understanding a language can open the gate, but what is on the other side is defined by something more complex called culture. That is, I think, what Calixte Duguay was trying to say very gently to those who cherish the French language. The question he was asking in his own way was, What does it mean to be Acadian? Is there an Acadian culture? And if there is, is it anything different than being a French-speaking New Brunswicker or a French-speaking Canadian? A French-speaking North American?

It used to be crystal clear to me. The culture of Grand Étang was, for me, the culture of all Acadie. And the culture of Grand Étang was bound up in the traditions, values, and ways of dealing with the world that had evolved over four hundred years. At its heart, Acadie was a peasant society where having degrees after your name didn't mean much, where being smart meant being able to use your head and hands to turn ideas into projects that could feed, clothe, and house your family. It meant figuring out how to build a sawmill at the bottom of a steep valley; how to use land carefully, sparingly, so that it returned the maximum bounty year after year. Everything was connected, not just people, but the seasons, the kind of land you owned, where and what you farmed. It was the kind of life where you could make a living from the land, but not make money.

A team of horses requires nothing more than hay you can grow yourself and shoes from the blacksmith a couple of times a year. In modern terms, the ratio of capital investment to production is phenomenally big. Ploughing, harrowing, hay cutting, timber cutting, a team of horses can do it all, but they can't compete with agribusiness.

In Cape Breton, the humble turnip was a bountiful, fail-proof crop and in the winter it fed both cattle and people; all vegetable peelings went to the sty to be eaten by the pigs; hens past laying were used to make a delicious coq au vin; the gum of the spruce tree was used to make spruce beer. Nothing was overlooked and nothing was wasted. If people lived today as my grandmother and grandfather lived in the first half of the twentieth century, the modern consumer economy would dissolve into a planetary pile of rusting cars and unused Nike/Coke/Gap products.

During the 1930s and '40s, when my uncles and aunts were growing up, Grandfather made two or three thousand dollars a year from the sale of cream and some summer construction work on the roads. He was considered to be doing well. His house and barn were always freshly painted; his children well fed and clothed. When unemployment insurance benefits became available from Ottawa, he refused to apply for them, even though he qualified from the summer road work, because he said the benefits were for workers in the city who had nothing but their jobs. He felt connected to them and did not want to take what he considered rightfully theirs. He did not consider himself to be unemployed in the winter. His employment just shifted.

Grandfather's farm was probably never more than a hundred acres, including the woodlot on the mountain, but he farmed it so knowledgeably that it fed ten children and earned a little money for the things that could not be made or grown or bartered. But this world has disappeared. Grand Étang's crab fishermen today make hundreds of thousands of dollars a season. Its educated children now work in Ottawa as lobbyists for global corporations. The village has three lawyers, lots of divorces, and a rather nice golf course. Times change. Cultures and people change.

I look around the hall in Richibucto at all these people searching for connections, but to what? To a genealogical paper trail? I leave the reunion with very mixed feelings. Perhaps I am expecting too much.

The world is a big place, and we each must sail on it in our own way. My cousin Roland has lived in Louisiana, Winnipeg, and Ottawa. But he's as rooted in the village of Grand Étang as ever. My children speak French, but their sense of themselves is as Canadians, not Acadians. And for me, my voyage has been, and always will be, to and from Acadie. It is where my soul most deeply connects to who I am.

I have come to realize that this cannot be explained. Identity is wrapped up in a complicated hierarchy of choices, and these choices are both arbitrary and free. I did not choose to be that little boy sitting at the kitchen table at his grandfather's. I did choose to say, *"Passez-moi le beurre, s'il vous plaît."* A sense of oneself intersects and connects with other people, great and small institutions, sometimes happily, sometimes painfully. Identity comes from many places, from both within and without, and cannot be reduced to a single moment, or explained like a multiplication table. Identity resists absolute definitions and often remains mysterious to both the owner and the stranger. This is why identity can be so explosive, for actions that challenge one's sense of self provoke immediate and visceral reactions.

My vision of Acadie and Acadians remains unchanged by the Retrouvailles. For me, what has made the Acadians important, what has made them more than just French-speaking New Brunswickers or French-speaking Canadians, is that they have continued to endure, to take care of each other, to be a distinctive people even without frontiers. For two and a half centuries Acadians have triumphed over distances, over borders, over poverty, over misfortune to keep in contact with each other, to keep Acadie alive beyond the boundaries of any particular village, town, province, or country. The importance of 1755 is not just that a great act of physical dispossession deprived a people of property but that the reason for that dispossession endures. As I write these words, there are long lines of people making their sorrowful way through a shattered landscape in Kosovo, hoping to find refuge somewhere, anywhere, else. The Acadian refugees of 1755 have different names, languages, and cultures in the twentieth century, but the fears and hatreds that are sending them into exile remain exactly the same. The twentieth century has been one of horror beyond anything known in the short history of humankind. In such a monstrous history of carnage, it is worth remembering a people who would not participate, who refused to bear arms on behalf of others.

This is the magic of Acadie and its gift to the world: a notion of inclusivity, of peaceful community, of caring for your neighbours. This was what the priest was talking about when he wrote to my father, before he left the village for university, saying that he was happy he was studying economics because it would give him new tools to help people; that this was what mattered.

As for me, in the end, all I can say is I am Acadian. My name is Clive à Fernand à William à Arsène à Magloire.

Epilogue

I have misplaced my plane ticket. I fumble around in various pockets while the Nordair flight threatens to take off for Kuujjuaq. In front of me, an Inuit woman holding a baby is arguing with the counter clerk. She is angry. She doesn't want to go to Kuujjuaq. She has no intention of going to Kuujjuaq; therefore, she doesn't need a ticket. She just wants to take the baby onto the plane and then return. The baby can travel free.

"Yes, but the baby must have someone to travel with," explains the clerk through gritted teeth. "She has to go on the plane with someone who has a ticket. It's simple. No ticket, no fly. It's against regulations."

"There is someone on the plane who will take the baby," says the Inuit woman, equally exasperated. "Someone who has a ticket." Then not so quietly under her breath to me, "Bitch! She's a bitch!"

The Nordair clerk responds by looking directly at me. She is going to ignore this woman with the baby. Just at that moment, I find my ticket and hand it to her over the heads of the Inuit woman and baby. The clerk processes my ticket promptly. The Inuit woman watches this transaction intently. I feel alarm bells going off. She wastes no time, she has made up her mind.

She turns to face me, blocking me from leaving the counter, and presents me with the baby. "You take the baby on the plane?" It's not so much a request as an order. She is a small woman but very determined. The alarm bells ring louder.

"I can't," I stammer. "I've got bags. I've got to meet the minister in Kuujjuaq."

"Good, you take the baby," she says more firmly. "He has a ticket," she says triumphantly to the clerk. Already she is passing the baby from her arms to mine.

"I can't." But the baby is now resting quietly in my arms.

"There's a woman on the plane," explains the Inuit woman. "A woman who will take the baby. You ask. She will be alone. This is a Clyde River baby. Very quiet. Very good."

This time it's my turn to ask for sympathy and support from the clerk, but her eyes have suddenly glazed over. The regulations have been satisfied. I have a ticket. The baby can go with a paying passenger.

The baby's face has red marks all over it. The Inuit woman explains that the baby has been "down south" in hospital. The baby is better now, she assures me. The red marks are new skin. The baby fell in a hot bowl of water, that's how it got burned. The Inuit woman explains this to me in the same very precise English that she used with the clerk.

She waves to me at the departure gate, and suddenly I am alone walking down a long corridor with a briefcase full of speeches and press releases for John Munro, the Minister of Indian Affairs, and a quiet, very good, Clyde River baby. By the time we get on the plane, the baby and I are conversing; mostly me talking and the baby listening. Babies make wonderful audiences. The stewardess smiles at me, and I remember it's not my baby. I explain my problem. The stewardess doesn't bat an eyelid and marches me down the aisle to where a young woman is sitting alone. We are quickly introduced. She is a northern child-care worker on her way to Frobisher Bay. My story makes perfect sense to her. She will take the Clyde River baby. I hand the baby and its bottle and blanket to her, a little awed by the calm with which the tiny infant slips from one arm to another.

I notice two colleagues from Indian Affairs sitting further down the aisle, engrossed in conversation. The plane pulls away from the loading dock. From my seat, I can hear the sing-song of Inuktitut, as well as the familiar chatter of English and French, as people settle into their places for the long trip. The little Inuit baby is right behind me with the child-care worker. In front of me there are two small children, blond haired and blue eyed. They're on their way to Frobisher Bay with their mother. To my right, I recognize Mary Simon, the president of Makivik Corporation, sitting with a companion. She is returning from a business trip to Montréal. Makivik is the Inuit corporation that, along with the Kativik regional government, runs much of Québec above the treeline. Parkas are stowed above and below the seats. The plane taxis down the runway, and with a great roar the plane hurls itself into the air.

The first-class section of the plane is loaded with freight. This is the only way supplies can get to Kuujjuaq during the freeze-up. It takes me a while to realize that I've been on a version of this flight before. It has the same feel as that of a country bus doing the milk run between Nova Scotia villages, except this one is at twenty-seven thousand feet above the earth and moving along at about six hundred miles an hour.

Nova Scotia, Acadie, the United States, Canada: identities and nations are created by people, not cosmic fiat. There is no rule that says particular countries must exist. History is littered with great nations that have come and gone. The Hittite empire flowered into a powerful civilization, powerful enough to conquer Egypt, and then disappeared four thousand years ago. The only guarantee in the universe is that there will not be stasis, that all things – including nations – will improve or decline, but they will not stay the same. What kind of nation are we building for that little baby from Clyde River? What kind of home?

I used to be confident about the kind of home that we were building in Canada and about the kind of world our leaders wanted. In my youth, I watched my father, who came from a tiny French-speaking village, rise to become the chairman of the Saltwater Fish Corporation and the adviser to cabinet ministers. I watched Canada's new red-and-white flag rise above the Peace Tower on Parliament Hill for the first time. I saw my father battle for, and succeed in getting, new harbour facilities for fishing villages. Medicare swept in from the West on the coattails of Tommy Douglas's notion that if everyone paid a little, no one would have to pay a lot. I watched the French language under Trudeau move from the back of the bus to share a place at the front. I heard Prime Minister Diefenbaker say no to the Americans' nuclear weapons, Pearson and Trudeau say no to the death penalty and the Vietnam War. I watched Canada enter the community of nations on its own terms in its own way. All of this before I was old enough to vote.

Things come together and apart – that seems to be the first law of the universe. Things came together for my father, not just for his career but in the larger sense: the kind of world that he believed in was reflected in the kinds of policies and programs that he worked for, whether from John Diefenbaker's Tories or Pierre Trudeau's Liberals. It hasn't been the same for me. Mostly, I've felt like a grunt soldier in a long and endless retreat. The governments of Mulroney and Chrétien feel exactly the same to me, but not in a way that I can support.

Small countries depend on the goodwill and grace of larger, more powerful countries to respect their boundaries and sense of difference. And small peoples within countries, such as the Acadians, such as the Métis, depend on there being harmony between their values and goals and those of the larger nation they are part of. The kind of nation that my grandfather felt comfortable in was the same kind of nation that Cree elder Roger Jones was addressing when he said Canada's new Constitution reflected none of the values that his people cherished – love, sharing, honesty, truth, the values that hold families, communities and, ultimately, nations together.

The enduring characteristic of Acadie is love of place and community. But the global capital that now runs the world has no home and no love except the law of the lowest price. If a government rises from a community of citizens that has no trust in anything but the lowest costs, the lowest taxes, court resolutions and a winning lawsuit, then how can that government cherish the kind of world that I want for myself and my children?

By today's measure, my grandfather was an antique when he refused to accept unemployment insurance during the winter. But it seemed pretty straightforward to him, being Canadian and Acadian were both about sharing with your neighbours.

I've learned that I can be exiled from a country without ever leaving. I can be exiled by the spirit of the times, but I've also learned that I can never be exiled from my kinship with all those who long for a better, more humane world. I hear the beat of that society in the songs of Paul Simon and the voice of Nelson Mandela. It is a voice that has no nationality, no colour, no accent. It is a place where the virtue of respect for the dignity of others takes precedence over money and advantage. As long as that voice and place exist, I will never be truly exiled, for their country is one I can share.

Through the airplane's porthole, I can see the arc of the planet's edge illuminated by a whiteness which does not look like anything that I have seen before. There is not enough colour for it to be sky. The curve of the earth flares cold and white, a bleach of ethereal light, above which there is only the darkness of space. Below, the Ottawa River curves through the Canadian Shield in a long, thin question mark. From thirty thousand feet it is the only landmark that I can recognize, then it, too, disappears into the white. The cold envelops the plane and I can feel it drilling through the plane's aluminum skin. The dull roar of the jets is the only thing between us and the endless mystery of space.